There was a child who was so mild
That no one thought of her as wild.
And yet beneath her gentle face
Was chaos time could not erase.

And every day her pain would stay
Just out of reach, in no one's way.
And though she smiled, her soul was riled
Because it had been long defiled.

Yet, unreleased, her pain increased
Until her deepest longings ceased.
And in her mind she built the kind
Of fortress no one else could find.

Now all alone, in walls of stone,
A young girl guards her fragile throne.
And nobody can hurt her there,
And nobody can show they care.

So pain presumptuously plods on
With fear the queen and rage the pawn.
They fight to shield and yet to free
The little girl I once called Me.

Front cover and poem
by
Anna Lyn Price

Supporting Ritual Abuse Survivors

by
Diane W. Hawkins, M.A.

For more information
please contact:

Restoration in Christ Ministries
PO Box 479, Grottoes, VA 24441-0479
540-298-2272

Copyright © 1995-2001
9th edition
Restoration in Christ Ministries
All Rights Reserved. No part of this book may be reproduced in any form, except for brief quotation in articles or reviews, without written permission from the publisher.

Published by
Restoration in Christ Ministries
PO Box 479
Grottoes, VA 24441-0479
540-298-2272
Fax 540-249-9716

ISBN 0-9708073-0-9
Library of Congress Control Number: 2001126138

Printed in the United States by
Morris Publishing
3212 East Highway 30
Kearney, NE 68847
1-800-650-7888

Dedication

*With love and appreciation
to my beloved husband
and greatest supporter,*
Tom

Table of Contents

Preface .... **ix**
Introduction **1**
Building Trust **7**
The Role of Conflict in DID **13**
    The Creation of Dissociative Barriers 13
    The Removal of Dissociative Barriers 18
    Implications for Relationship 20
Emotional Support **21**
    The Nature of Repressed Emotions 21
    Confusion about Emotions 22
    Processing Memories 27
    Anger 31
    Guilt 34
    Fear 35
    Processing Current Life Experiences 37
Physical Support **39**
    Protection from Self Harm 39
    Assistance with Daily Living 42
Spiritual Support **45**
    Prayer 45
    Spiritual Warfare 46
    Bible Study and Discipleship 52
Financial Support **55**
Therapeutic Support **57**

Supporting Versus Caretaking **59**
The Role of the Church **61**
Spiritual Protection **67**
    The Belt of Truth 70
    The Breastplate of Righteousness 73
    The Boots of Peace 75
    The Shield of Faith 84
    The Helmet of Salvation 88
    The Sword of the Spirit 89
    Conclusion 89

Appendices
A. Definition of Terms **91**
B. Types of Alter-Personalities **99**
C. Requirements for Types of Support **101**
D. A Plan for Implementing an SRA Support Team within the Local Church **107**
E. Satanic Calendar **111**

Endnotes **113**

Preface

As a ritual abuse survivor myself, I write this book from an inside perspective, not because I have received significant support in my own healing journey, but because I know how important it is. Too often the diagnosis we bear leads to a tremendous sense of isolation in a world that has no "box" in which to fit us. Building any kind of a relationship usually requires that we live behind an artificial mask, trying our best to conceal the dynamics of who we really are and the struggles that are so real in our lives. This book is an effort on my part to help bridge this information gap, building understanding that will hopefully result in greater support for those who are courageously fighting to reclaim lives which have been shattered by unspeakable evil.

I have drawn the contents of the book not only from my own personal experience but also from my observations and interactions with scores of other survivors whom I have met in various types of therapy groups as well as through my involvement with Restoration in Christ Ministries, which is devoted almost entirely to addressing the needs of ritual abuse survivors. **I have chosen to use the feminine gender throughout the book simply for the purpose of smoother reading. While the majority of abuse survivors seeking healing are indeed female, in actual fact males are victims of ritualistic and other forms of abuse just as frequently. However, they are less apt to acknowledge it and seek treatment.**

Because I am a Christian and believe that God is an essential resource in all emotional healing, I cannot help but write from a

Christian perspective. While non-Christians can offer significant support to survivors, Christians can offer even more because of their direct relationship to God and His divine resources.

While originally designed to bring understanding and guidance to supporters of ritual abuse survivors, this book is proving to be extremely instructive and affirming to survivors themselves, especially in the early stages of therapy. Furthermore, although ritual abuse survivors generally manifest the most complex dynamics, much of the material in this book applies equally well to non-SRA (Satanic Ritual Abuse) multiples or abuse survivors in general.

Appendix A contains a glossary of terms which are commonly associated with Dissociative Identity Disorder (DID) and is designed to assist those readers who are unfamiliar with this psychological diagnosis. I particularly draw your attention to my definition of "cult" and "cultist," which I use in a slightly uncustomary way in this book.

I deeply appreciate the use of Anna Lyn Price's artwork on the cover and her accompanying poem, the cover lay-out design by Sheila Salmon, the formatting help from my husband, Tom, and the gracious assistance in proof reading by Juli Kuhl and Scott Moose. Juli also helped significantly in giving me the courage to submit the book for publication without it reaching my own standard of perfection.

I trust that you will find the book helpful in explaining some of the complex dynamics involved in Dissociative Identity Disorder and ritual abuse. As understanding and acceptance continue to grow, survivors can emerge from the shadows and more readily receive the help and support they so desperately need.

Supporting Ritual Abuse Survivors

Introduction

Due to the exponential growth of generational Satanism and the natural aging of the many Baby Boomers who were innocently subjected to post-World War II mind control experiments, the last two decades have seen increasing numbers of ritual abuse survivors seeking help. Accomplishing the covert agendas of the perpetrators involved in these activities usually required having individuals whose minds were split into separate identities, a condition attainable only by inflicting severe trauma at a young age. The survivors of this coercive and manipulative form of abuse therefore suffer from what is now known as Dissociative Identity Disorder (DID).

Formerly called Multiple Personality Disorder, DID is a unique psychological condition in which the mind splits itself into separate identities in order to cope with overwhelming childhood trauma. Amnestic barriers are generally erected between the alter-identities, or "alters," who are formed to enable some parts of the person to maintain a sense of normalcy in an otherwise intolerable situation. These protected identities are able to function in everyday life without being encumbered with the effects of the abuse.

The resulting separation of consciousness benefits not only the survivors, but also the perpetrators, providing an ideal cover for their secret, and often criminal, acts. Once the amnestic barriers are in place, they can intimidate, indoctrinate, program, and use the split-off parts for their own purposes, and the "presenting alters," who normally handle everyday life, will be totally amnestic to their hideous acts, maintaining an innocent silence and revealing few clues of abuse.

Research reveals that only a very immature mind will respond to extreme trauma by creating separate identities. DID therefore occurs only in individuals whose trauma *began* before the age of five or six. Once the mind initiates this type of defense, however, it can continue to create more alter-identities throughout life—whenever it serves a beneficial purpose.

While the majority of DID cases arises from a deliberately orchestrated splitting of the mind for specific cultic purposes, this is not always the case. A young mind can split into multiple identities in the face of *any kind* of overwhelming trauma. Clinicians have observed, however, that over 90% of cases generally involve some form of early sexual abuse.

Rather than being a true mental illness, DID actually represents a marvelously creative defense mechanism employed by extremely traumatized children. When they had no way of *external* escape, they found a way to escape the intolerable events *internally*. The condition bears the negative connotation of "disorder" only because its smooth operation often breaks down later in life. Disturbing memories, emotions, and behaviors begin seeping through weakened dissociative barriers, interfering with normal daily living and alerting the Host personality that something is wrong. This is what usually motivates survivors to seek help.

Thankfully, DID is treatable in the hands of a knowledgeable therapist and with the proper motivation and cooperation of the survivor. The journey to healing and wholeness is generally a long and grueling process, however. It requires facing, owning, and processing the seemingly unbearable events as well as resolving the psychological conflicts arising from them. In cases of ritual abuse, varying degrees of mind-control programming and demonization are also involved and further complicate the healing process.

A skilled therapist trained in dealing with these specialized issues is generally needed to facilitate the recovery process. Clinicians clearly recognize, however, that survivors progress more quickly when they have some form of support to draw upon outside of their therapy sessions. Many openly acknowledge how important the component of *love* is to the healing process.

What a profound opportunity for growth and blessing this offers to those who are willing to provide love and support for one of God's deeply damaged children seeking healing from such a sordid past! While serving in such a role is not necessarily easy, your performance anxieties may be significantly relieved if you remember that your main objective is to provide a channel of love into her life. If you are a Christian and allow God and His love to fill *your* life, you will have a tremendous impact on the survivor. Admittedly, not everyone is suited for such a role, but God will certainly make His resources abound for those He calls or places in such a situation.

Drawing upon human resources to increase your knowledge of DID and ritual abuse, its effects on survivors, and their particular needs during the recovery process is also beneficial. Reading materials and attending seminars on the subject as well as consulting with others more familiar with the diagnosis will enable you to make a more knowledgeable decision concerning entering a support relationship, or if you are already involved, it will greatly enhance your effectiveness. The more informed you are, the less likely you are to be derailed by unexpected surprises.

Supporting a ritual abuse survivor is likely to stretch you in many ways. Spiritually, it may expand your current conception of evil and test your faith in God and His power and goodness as never before. The more you assist a survivor to free herself from bondage to the powers of darkness, the more Satan may try to work against you. For this reason a strong relationship with God is vitally important as well as a confident grasp of the principles of spiritual warfare. Remember that whatever God requires of you will be matched by His all-sufficient supply of grace, strength, wisdom, and love!

God will also not leave you unrewarded. He will undoubtedly use the challenges you face to mature and refine your character for His glory and to lead you to a deeper understanding of Himself and the spiritual realm (James 1:2-3; 1 Peter 1:6-7). You will also participate in the thrill of victory as you watch the power of God triumph over evil, releasing the survivor from the powers of darkness and providing deep inner healing through Jesus Christ. This joy will be beyond compare—to say nothing of the reward awaiting you in heaven from Jesus Himself (Mark 9:31; Matthew 25:40).

When you commit yourself to supporting a survivor on her journey to healing, the benefits she reaps will be immeasurable. She may never have had a friendship governed by unconditional love in which she can feel a sense of safety and security. Her experience with you may rekindle her ability to start trusting others and perhaps even increase her faith in God's love for her. Because she has most likely grown up in a dysfunctional home, she will undoubtedly benefit from the mentoring that you can offer her in many areas. Helping her grow in responsibility, accountability, boundary setting, and self-care will be invaluable to her success in life.

"Multiples" (people with multiple identities) vary greatly in the nature and extent of support that they require. While some are very capable individuals performing at a professional level, others are quite disabled functionally. Most lie somewhere in between these extremes. Even those who appear so "together," however, carry tremendous pain, inner conflict, and turmoil beneath their external facade. They are just better able to separate, or dissociate, from it in order to function.

Marital status is another factor affecting the degree of support a particular multiple needs. In general, those who are living on their own without any kind of healthy support from their families need considerably more involvement from support persons. If a married survivor's spouse is not handling her diagnosis well or is dysfunctional, abusive, or frequently absent for whatever reason, she will also have increased needs for support. Even having an understanding and supportive spouse does not eliminate a survivor's need for additional external support, however.

The level of neediness and dysfunction within any multiple may vary along the journey as well. Don't expect a steady uphill climb marked by consistent improvements. Setbacks can occur at any stage of the process. When therapy gets intense, both emotions and functionality can nose-dive. At other times a single internal victory may produce profound improvement almost overnight.

The gifts and capabilities of potential support people vary too, and this is just as important to recognize. God has purposely gifted each one differently in the Body and therefore desires to use us in different roles as well. In the broad scope of support needs described in this book, you may feel comfortable and capable of giving certain kinds of support but not others. The most ideal situation is for a survivor to have a *team* of supporters so that the members can complement each other in their roles and no one gets burned out.

Potential supporters must also consider the status of their own journey though life. If you are dealing with heavy issues of your own, you may not have the emotional capacity to become deeply involved with a multiple, or you may have to limit yourself to specific types of support that require little emotional involvement. You should also be aware that supporting a multiple through her abuse issues may bring issues of your own to the forefront. If this occurs, remember that taking care of yourself is equally as important as ministering to the survivor's needs. Do not try to be a super-hero or a martyr. Thank God for using this situation to bring to your attention things that need to be addressed in your own life, and take the time to do so. I truly believe that most survivors will understand this.

The availability of time is another variable in the lives of potential support people which must be considered. If you do commit yourself to a survivor, you will need to set firm boundaries so that your own needs, the needs of your family, and your other responsibilities will not be neglected. In doing so, you will model proper self-care, which is usually a critical area in which abuse survivors need to grow.

Building Trust

Trust doesn't come easily if you were repeatedly hurt by those you trusted as a child. Therefore, developing any kind of close relationship with another person can be a scary thing for an abuse survivor. Many find themselves caught in a conflict in which they long to have a supportive, caring relationship but at the same time are very frightened by that prospect.

As a potential supporter, you need to understand this fear and recognize that learning to trust again may come slowly for a survivor. Therefore, be careful not to push yourself on one too fast as this will usually heighten her fears and defenses. Be gentle, patient, and sensitive to how far she opens the door to you.

Learning to trust again is a very necessary component of the healing process, however. Survivors obviously have to trust a therapist in order to reveal to him or her the very depths of their beings. Hopefully they will also be willing to trust others, especially those whom God may graciously send to walk alongside them on their journey.

Like most people, the way survivors evaluate trustworthiness is greatly affected by their personal history. Their abuse not only tinted the glasses through which they view people but usually resulted in the development of incredible "radar" for reading people. You may therefore find yourself being scrutinized as never before.

Their carefully attuned antennae will be particularly sensitive to anything that likens you to their perpetrators, whether it be physical attributes, particular mannerisms, or character traits. Obviously some of these things are totally irrational harbingers of fear, but they will nevertheless evoke this response in the survivor because of her history.

She may eventually be able to recognize that and overcome these unfounded fears, but she will need your patience and understanding as she does. Even valid indicators of trustworthiness will be of heightened importance to her because of how she was hurt so deeply by their absence in the past.

Abuse often leads to a deeply rooted belief that actions are a much more reliable indicator of reality than words. Therefore, in her initial evaluation a survivor is apt to note very carefully how your actions match the words you speak. Only when she is convinced of their consistency will she begin trusting your words alone.

Abuse survivors have been deceived—and hurt—many times by people who appeared to be nice on the surface. Therefore they will generally focus their attention primarily on character issues, which reveal the true person, rather than relying on superficialities. They know all too well that "bad guys" can dress well, talk smoothly, and give out candy.

Heading the list of character traits that will help to win their trust is **moral integrity** with its many corollaries. This was totally absent or utterly inconsistent in their abusers. In fact, some may not even know what true moral integrity looks like in a person. They do know, however, how much they were hurt by people who constantly deceived them and had no regard to any standard of human decency and respect. They therefore have virtually no tolerance for any kind of duplicity, deception, or disregard for their personhood. For them, a trustworthy relationship must be marked by absolute **honesty** as well as **respect** and **kindness**. Because many have never experienced it, being treated with respect, and even dignity, is often an awesome "door opener" for trust and a new kind of relationship.

Consistency is also of heightened importance to them in light of how inconsistently their abusers treated them. Just as your words and actions must match, so must the way you treat them from day to day. Therefore, if you decide to change the dynamics of the relationship, be sure to inform them of this as well as your reasons for the change.

Dependability is equally important. This means following through with whatever plans or promises you make—or carefully explaining why you couldn't. Unexpected changes are particularly unsettling because of how often in their childhood this heralded the onset of trauma.

Openness is another crucial quality. They have too often been deeply hurt by the sly manipulations and deceptions of their perpetrators. Therefore if they detect anything going on behind their backs, it can strike terror in their hearts! Some may even find it difficult to trust that a secret can ever be meant for their good. They may have to learn what you mean by a "good secret."

Firm moral and personal boundaries are extremely important for two reasons. First of all, because they have had their boundaries violated so much in the past, survivors are usually supersensitive to any inappropriate or uninvited intrusion into their "personal space." People who try to come too close too soon make them uncomfortable. On the other hand, they need *others* to have firm boundaries because sometimes they have no idea where boundaries should be placed. So they have parts who overreact in opposite directions regarding boundaries—but that's what DID is all about!

A quality which really impresses survivors is a willingness to **acknowledge mistakes.** While they generally want you to be perfect—at the other end of the performance spectrum from their abusers—to a certain extent they realize that you can't be. So acknowledging when you "goof" will go a long way in redeeming yourself in their eyes. None of their abusers ever did that!

Sensitivity is also important. Although their abuse often hardened them to endure extraordinary physical adversity, it has left most survivors supersensitive emotionally. The slightest hint of mistreatment may tap into deep, unhealed wounds and evoke a major reaction emotionally. Protector alters may emerge to defend them or to retaliate in an aggressive manner. Sensitivity is needed not only to avoid setting off such a reaction, but also to handle the situation when it occurs.

Because of their traumatic childhoods, survivors have other alters with distorted, negative views of life and people too. You will need particular sensitivity to relate to them in a validating manner which doesn't reinforce their negative perceptions but instead opens the door to constructive dialogue.

Torturous abuse unfortunately leaves its victims with a host of irrational fears and peculiar reactions to seemingly innocuous things. Some of these were deliberately programmed into them while others are a natural aftermath of the terrifying things to which they were subjected. While you cannot possibly be sensitive to all of their "triggers" before you know them, your handling them delicately when you *do* become aware of them means a lot. Through genuine understanding and support you may even be able to assist them in gaining victory over these troublesome reactions.

Developing sensitivity in all of these areas will take time. In some you may learn by mistakes, but if you can maintain a teachable spirit and allow the survivor to fill you in on what went wrong, the relationship will probably not be damaged.

Compassion is another critical attribute for a support person. While survivors may recognize your legitimate need to set boundaries on the extent of your emotional involvement with them, they need to feel that you are genuinely moved by their history of horrific abuse even if you choose not to know the details of it. If you maintain too cold or aloof an attitude, you will rarely get in the front door with them. They will be too apt to read your extreme emotional detachment as disbelief or judgment.

Your **non-judgmental acceptance of all their alters** is also important. Although as a support person you will not necessarily meet every one of them, you never know who may emerge in a given situation. They are not all naturally amicable or endowed with social graces. While some are happy, carefree, and delightful, others may be angry, vulgar, aggressive, seductive, or deeply withdrawn. You may be surprised to meet alters of both sexes among their company of "selves" as well as a wide span of ages. All of this may be difficult to comprehend initially, but hopefully you will quickly adjust and be able to welcome and relate equally well to whomever appears.

Accepting each of a survivor's alters is vital for several reasons. First of all, distinguishing alters as "good" or "bad" enhances internal conflict and perpetuates the need for their ongoing separation. Secondly, judgment or rejection closes the door of opportunity for influencing change in their perspectives and behaviors. Finally, by readily accepting all of their alters, you become a powerful model to them. If they are ever to reunite with all of them, the process begins with acceptance—and sometimes that's hard for them too.

Closely related to acceptance is having **respect for each alter's contribution**. Always remember that whatever their surface presentation may be, every alter serves a protective purpose. When you probe into the history of the most obnoxious or antagonistic alters, you will learn the crucial role they played in the person's survival, often taking on the worst abuse in order to spare the Core. Keeping this in mind will greatly enhance your appreciation and respect for them.

While demonstrating these qualities will usually provide a solid foundation for a survivor's trust, in some cases the fear of trust may be so strong that she is unable to overcome it, no matter how trustworthy you prove yourself to be. In these instances she may need gentle assistance in challenging her beliefs and the bases of her fears.

If you have the opportunity, try to help her see that although her fear is legitimate and understandable in light of her personal history, it is depriving her of desirable benefits now. Just because she was consistently hurt as a child by those she tried to trust, this is not true *all* the time with *all* people. You might try pointing out others who seemingly enjoy relationships of trust without getting hurt. Challenge her to move from applying her fear of trust globally to *all* people in *all* situations to learning how to assess which people are trustworthy and which are not. Sometimes she may have to process some of her memories of when her trust was painfully betrayed and get healing for those wounds before trust will be able to grow again. Therefore, encourage her to discuss her fear of trust with her therapist.

Whatever the situation, don't ever force yourself into a relationship with a survivor. Respect her viewpoint if she, for some reason, does not feel comfortable or safe in pursuing it. Having a *choice* is a precious thing to a survivor, and learning to utilize it is often a major step in the healing process too.

Even when a survivor responds positively to you, proceed slowly and cautiously. Recognize that this relationship will be much more complex than any you have previously experienced. Because of this, both survivor and support person do well to wade into it gradually.

The Role of Conflict in DID

Understanding the role which conflict plays in the dynamics of DID will enhance your ability to interact with multiples and their system of alter-identities in a manner that is most conducive to their healing. It will help you appreciate the distinct perspectives and roles of the alters and know how to validate them in an appropriate way that facilitates the eventual removal of the dissociative walls between them rather than strengthening them.

The Creation of Dissociative Barriers

While DID is created in a child's mind as a means to cope with extreme trauma, escaping the physical pain or overwhelming emotions is probably not the primary motivating factor in the splitting process. Rather, the child seems to use dissociation as an ingenious way to resolve what she perceives as intolerable conflicts arising *from* the trauma.

Psychological conflicts exist whenever a person feels two or more opposing needs, beliefs, or feelings at the same time. When the conflict involves seemingly *inviolable* needs or beliefs, the conflict becomes intolerable and requires a drastic defense by the psyche. If this seemingly intolerable conflict occurs in the early years of life, the mind often has the capacity to resolve the situation through dissociation—extreme dissociation which results in the splitting of the mind into separate identities.

For instance, if Daddy brutally hurts or molests his child, this creates an intolerable conflict with the child's inherent belief that she needs a protective parent in order to survive. Because she cannot psychologically cope with this reality which conflicts with her inviolable belief concerning survival, she splits herself so that her Core Self can remain amnestic to the event and thus maintain the belief that she has the kind of parents who will assure her survival while a separate identity bears the reality of the abuse.

If you can grasp the mechanism of this most foundational conflict in producing alter-identities, you will understand that whenever the psyche of the young child believes that it is in an unsurvivable situation, it will use the means of dissociation, or "splitting," to protect the Core from knowledge of the event in order to maintain its confidence of survival. The more the child is placed in situations that threaten this critical belief, the more alter-identities she will possibly create to separate the trauma from her normal stream of consciousness.

Perhaps the strength of this basic survival conflict diminishes with age and this is why DID is rarely produced when severe trauma is first encountered after the age of five or six. Perhaps by then children have a greater sense of autonomy and no longer view themselves as being so dependent on a caretaker for survival.

However, children who have already begun to split themselves into alter-identities may face additional conflicts over the course of their lives that seem just as intolerable. Generally their minds will revert to the same dissociative mechanism to cope with these conflicts as well, splitting themselves again and again to separate the two or more opposing needs, beliefs, or feelings into separate alters.

For instance, as such children mature, they will undoubtedly be required to take on increasing responsibilities in caring for themselves, participating in family life, and going to school. This eventually creates a critical situation if they are also experiencing frequent abuse. In such cases the psyche seemingly tries to protect the "unabused" Core from significant involvement in external life. However, putting the trauma-bearing alters into functioning roles is equally unacceptable. Not only are they generally too laden down with the emotional impact of the abuse to be able to function normally, but it would defeat the whole purpose of keeping the trauma memories separated from normal consciousness.

The demand for normal functioning therefore places upon the Core an intolerable conflict between the simultaneous needs to protect itself and yet to perform normally.

This conflict generally produces another major splitting from the Core. The newly formed identity will be just as separated from the knowledge and implications of the trauma as the Core, thereby enabling the child to live a seemingly normal, consistent life in all the settings in which this is required. This new identity is called the Host, and while directly related to the Core, functions separately from her.

This has now effectively divided the psyche of the child into three major components: the Core, who resists owning the truth for the purpose of survival; the Host, who resists owning the truth for the purpose of functioning; and the large group of alter-identities who contain the trauma memories so that the Core and Host can both maintain their illusion that no abuse happened. Virtually every multiple will exhibit these three major divisions in their psyches as the underlying conflicts which create them are generally universal in cases of repeated, severe abuse.

Other intolerable conflicts causing further splitting of the psyche will depend on the particular circumstances the individual encounters. Not all will arise directly out of trauma, as illustrated in the creation of the Host. Some will arise naturally while others may be deliberately orchestrated by knowledgeable perpetrators who desire to produce the strong amnestic barriers which are essential for their covert purposes.

Naturally occurring conflicts may involve such things as the control of forbidden emotions. Anger, for instance, is a natural emotional response to abuse; yet any display of it is usually strictly prohibited by the abuser. This extremely common conflict generally results in the creation of an alter-identity to hold the anger so that other identities can remain anger-free.

Another typical conflict many abused children confront is the inability to meet the performance standard they perceive is necessary to avoid further pain. If they are also severely shamed for their failure to perform well, their sense of inherent "goodness" becomes tied to the unattainable performance standard as well. When these children perceive no other way to escape the intolerable punishment or chastisement, they often resolve the conflict by further splitting.

This conflict often results in the creation of a new identity who truly believes that she is perfect and therefore both safe and "good." She usually reflects a positive attitude and a strong self-image, perhaps accompanied by some veiled feelings of superiority. However, she experiences life only when the person's behavior is truly in line with the perceived requirements of the perpetrator(s) so that she can maintain her illusion of perfection.

The alter(s) left to deal with the reality of imperfection may become compulsively devoted to an ever-increasing list of rules gleaned from their astute observation of the perpetrator(s) as well as society in general. Every aspect of the survivor's life may be governed by these rigid, often self-imposed, directives, which gain their strength from the belief that she will be okay if she can just do everything "right" on a consistent basis. The Host will generally feel this underlying compulsion but not understand its origin.

If the person repeatedly fails to measure up in the eyes of the perpetrator(s) in spite of her heroic efforts, she will be confronted with the unbearable reality that rule-keeping will *not* keep her safe or make her "good." Because she cannot tolerate this reality and its perceived consequences, she may generate another split so that she can still maintain the more tolerable illusion that rule-keeping will both keep her safe and make her morally acceptable while the new identity carries the inevitability of failure. This part may exhibit a fatalistic gloom and complete loss of motivation for life. She may see herself as inexorably "bad," unable to measure up, and deserving of the severe punishment she receives from her abuser(s). Feeling totally void of human worth or value, she is apt to become quite suicidal.

Other intolerable conflicts arise when survivors are forced into an activity which is totally against the moral standards or spiritual commitments of the Core. In this case a new identity will be created to handle the absolutely unacceptable activity (e.g., illicit sex, perpetrator acts, or criminal activity) so the primary identities can maintain the belief that they do not do such things. The alter embodying the immoral behavior will generally adopt a non-dissociative means to lessen its repulsive impact, such as viewing herself to be of the opposite sex or taking on the belief system of the perpetrator(s).

When you meet this alter, she may seem to have a very seared conscience, and you may be tempted to judge her for her immoral perspectives or behavior. If, however, you understand the intolerable conflict which her existence is serving to resolve and how this protects the Core from owning what is so objectionable to her, you will be much more apt to treat her with compassion. Rather than judgment, she needs guidance in recognizing the nature of the conflict out of which she was created and help in working with the Core to resolve it in a manner that ends the need for dissociation. This will, of course, entail a major change on the part of the Core because she will have to accept what to her was totally unacceptable.

Because cult perpetrators understand the role of conflict in producing dissociation, they intentionally manipulate the lives of their subjects to create strong conflicts. They are extremely adept at this and realize that the more intense the conflict, the stronger will be the dissociative (and amnestic) barriers erected to separate the parts of the person holding the opposing views.

This is perhaps one reason they like to work with children from Christian homes. The stronger a person's Christian commitment is, the stronger will be the barriers separating them from the identities which are forced into immoral, criminal, or Satanic activity—which is exactly what they want in order to keep their cover in place. These are the identities from which they can then build entire systems of alters who can be manipulated to serve their own purposes.

Sometimes highly organized perpetrator groups even train cooperating parents to raise their children in a way that accentuates these conflicts. This may include setting unreasonably high performance standards for them at home as well as attending legalistic churches, where they will be taught an excessive number of rules for "God pleasing" behavior along with the severe consequences of breaking them. Sometimes these parents may teach their children strict adherence to extreme moral values and severely assassinate the character of those who violate them. This sets the child up for an intense psychological conflict when she is then forced by her perpetrator(s) to violate these standards herself.

The Removal of Dissociative Barriers

The dissociative barriers created by these severe conflicts will remain in place until the two seemingly incompatible needs, beliefs, or realities are identified, challenged, and resolved. This usually involves having the identities separated by the conflict return to the memory of the event in which the split occurred and challenge the beliefs underlying the conflict and seemingly necessitating the split. When these beliefs are adjusted to reflect truth (see "Processing Memories," p. 28), the conflict may resolve itself quickly, making the dissociative walls separating them no longer necessary.

To an outside observer the beliefs needing to be changed may seem so obviously irrational and the process of correcting them relatively simple. Remember, however, that the primary identities originally viewed the events in question as absolutely intolerable. Therefore, without careful handling, broaching these issues again could cause another drastic response by the psyche. Survivors who have publicly recanted their stories and even sued their therapists for implanting false memories may have been pushed too far too fast, threatening their treasured belief systems beyond their ability to cope.

In order for the Core identity to own the events she has resisted owning for so many years, her threshold of tolerance must somehow be raised at a deep psychological level. In addition, she must be willing to give up the tremendous advantages she has enjoyed by being sheltered from the reality of her abuse. These include her separation from the debilitating pain, guilt, and shame associated with these events; her untainted moral image of herself; and her belief in the basic goodness of mankind and safety of the world in which she lives. What strength and courage it will take for her to make these major sacrifices!

Daring to move out of her protective shell and embrace the history, behavior, and personalities of all her alter-identities means coming to grips not only with the things she did, but also with the reality of who she is. The identity crisis this precipitates is extremely far-reaching, encompassing her personality, her capabilities, her family, her childhood, her morality, her sexual purity, and her spirituality. Without being in her shoes, you cannot possibly comprehend the enormity of this challenge!

If the survivor has always seen herself as a self-confident and outgoing person, owning the parts of her who are depressed and withdrawn may be difficult. Likewise, if she knows herself only as a high functioning person, she may resist accepting that "she" is sometimes weak, confused, and has to struggle to get things done.

Embracing her full history will abolish any belief that she may have had of a normal, happy childhood. If her family was involved in her abuse, she will have to come to grips with the dreaded reality that those who gave her birth and were supposed to love and protect her, betrayed her instead.

The issues involving the survivor's personal morality may be the toughest hurdles of her journey to wholeness. Try to imagine the magnitude of the shock that she will experience if she has always viewed herself as a moral, law-abiding citizen and must suddenly embrace the reality that she has participated in unspeakable acts of immorality and crime? What if these include torturing or sacrificing other humans, maybe her own siblings or children?

She will be equally as affected if she has thoroughly committed herself to maintaining sexual purity and must suddenly accept that she has been sexually violated by perhaps many people, at times with her seeming consent, and even entered into blood covenants with them. If she is deeply devoted to God, she will have just as much difficulty accepting that she has participated in rituals and sacrifices to Satan or other deities—and probably has allowed extensive demonization to occur as well.

I hope this gives you a slight idea of what pulling back the curtain and meeting one's true identity means. Perhaps you will better understand the enormity of that step and recognize the degree of ego strength, inner motivation, and support that must be in place for a survivor to consider doing that. Those who make it are truly heroes!

While the requirements for achieving unity in place of dissociation are enormous, nothing is impossible with God! He is able to wrap the survivor in His arms of love and accompany her with His supernatural strength every step of the way. He knows how to provide truth in just the way she needs it to overcome every hurdle and be set free from the many bondages crippling her life. As the walls begin to come down and she begins claiming more and more of her true self, she will experience a deep sense of "rightness" about the process and this will help to propel her forward until she is completely whole.

Implications for Relationship

From the beginning of the survivor's journey, the way you relate to her and her alter-identities will have a profound impact on either strengthening or weakening the conflicts which seemingly necessitate the dissociative barriers. A key principle to understand regarding any conflict is that the stronger one side advances its beliefs or agenda, the stronger the other side will assert its beliefs. For instance, when evidence is encountered to support the allegations of those alters holding the memories of the abuse, the parts invested in denial may proclaim their position even more strongly. If they are too threatened, they may take drastic action, such as making a friendly visit to the perpetrator or even withdrawing from therapy.

You must therefore be careful not to strengthen the position of any particular side of a conflict. This often means withholding your perspective and revealing no favoritism toward either side. Whenever you give the impression that one side is "right" and the other "wrong," you further incite one side against the other and strengthen the ongoing need to keep them separate.

As much as possible, show equal respect to every personality regardless of their characteristics. Avoid labels which subtly imply judgment, such as "light side" or "dark side." Be particularly careful not to support the Core/Host's condemnation of "sinful" alters. Not only will this strengthen the wall between them, but it also may drive the scorned ones into deeper hiding, which is counterproductive to healing. Instead, convey a willingness to hear the perspective of all parts.

Because these conflict-reducing responses are often the opposite of what comes naturally, don't expect immediate perfection from yourself. As time progresses, these principles will sink in and gradually become more spontaneous, resulting in significant benefit to the survivor.

Emotional Support

Supporting a ritual abuse survivor through the emotional throes of her recovery process is one of the most appreciated and healing forms of support you can offer. It is probably the most challenging and potentially draining to the supporter as well. Those able to assist in this area need a special sensitivity to hurting people; substantial inner fortitude; and a good grasp of the dynamics of trauma, emotions, and dissociation.

If you are willing to accompany the survivor as she revisits the unbearable memories of her past, your presence alone will speak volumes, contrasting greatly with the utter abandonment she felt when the events originally took place. Your compassion will wash over her deep inner wounds like a medicinal balm, and she will at last receive what she so badly needed and deserved as a child.

Because the mind will only release its painful hidden secrets if it senses that the person is in a safe and supportive environment, you may be the key that unlocks this important door which is so crucial to her healing. If you also learn the principles for bringing healing to those wounds once they are exposed, you will be of invaluable assistance to her.

The Nature of Repressed Emotions

Abuse invariably evokes intense emotions, no matter how or when it is inflicted. When it occurs in childhood, however, the individual generally lacks the opportunity to express or process those emotions as they arise. The perpetrator is too powerful. If the child were to react in anger or cry out in pain, she might risk greater punishment or torture.

Furthermore, any possibility of seeking comfort or confiding in another caring person is usually banished by severe threats against ever revealing what happened.

Most severely abused children therefore have no other option than to lock those feelings away from their conscious awareness and carry them unresolved into their adult lives. In DID the unacceptable emotions may be relegated to certain alters who have limited interaction with the external world.

Wherever they are hidden, those unresolved emotions never disappear permanently. While they may appear to lie completely dormant, their energy is often diverted into physical channels, causing a variety of psychosomatic ailments. In most cases they will eventually burst through their confining walls and emerge, perhaps decades later, with the same emotional force they carried in the beginning. However, because of the many intervening years their true source may not be readily evident.

Confusion about Emotions

Their Expression

Understanding a survivor's emotions can be quite confusing, especially at the beginning of treatment. At one extreme she may seem unusually devoid of emotions, not only in speaking of her abuse but in current situations as well. This is generally because she is still living under the deep childhood conviction that emotions are unacceptable. For the sake of safety she has continued to divert her naturally occurring emotions to a subconscious level and therefore appears totally unaffected by them.

At the other extreme a survivor may experience sporadic episodes of intense, seemingly inappropriate emotions which cause significant problems in her life and personal relationships. While this generally results in much blame being cast on her, these seemingly unnatural outbursts are quite explainable. She has just reached the point at which the dissociative barriers separating her from her long-buried emotions are weakening. Therefore, whenever a current incident bears even the slightest resemblance to an unresolved, anger-provoking event of the past, the minor emotional reaction to the current incident opens the door to the hidden reservoir of anger stored up from the past, giving it the opportunity to release some of its energy as well.

Once this dynamic is understood and recognized, the survivor can often make a special effort to direct the force of her reactions at the past atrocities instead of the current irritants. This usually makes life significantly better for those around her.

Lying in between these two extremes, some survivors may feel what I call "whispering ghosts" of their buried emotions. They may live with a nebulous cloud of gloom engulfing them most of the time or have a tendency to cry easily or for no apparent reason. Others may demonstrate an almost constant irritability or edginess. In most cases, however, the survivor is totally unaware that these niggling emotions are seeping into her consciousness from the huge internal reservoir to which she has relegated the powerful emotions connected to her abuse.

Another subtle and confusing way in which repressed emotions sneak out from their buried crypts is through what is called "transference." Webster defines "transference" as "the redirection of feelings and desires . . . unconsciously retained from childhood toward a new object," such as a therapist or a spouse.[1] In other words, the difficulties a survivor has in current relationships may be directly linked to unresolved issues she carries from similar relationships in her childhood.

While she genuinely perceives the problem to lie totally in the current situation, she is viewing it through her tainted childhood glasses, which greatly distort the nature and severity of the issues involved. She is, in fact, transferring her childhood patterns of feeling about, acting towards, or responding to a particular problem figure of her past onto the "offensive" contemporary. While some point of similarity between the past and present figures usually exists, thereby triggering the transference, the reaction is usually blown way out of proportion to reality.

For instance, if a survivor feels utter condemnation when her husband disagrees with her or rejection when her therapist establishes a new boundary in their relationship, she is probably transferring the context of past incidents, when these responses were legitimate, onto the present situation. Because she felt so condemned or rejected by a significant person in her childhood, she subconsciously attaches these feelings to the somewhat similar actions of individuals in her current life.

Sometimes the husband or therapist can be in a "no win" situation. Whatever he or she does may be viewed with contempt or suspicion by the survivor because of the nature of a past relationship. Until she can resolve the issues of that relationship or somehow differentiate the present dynamics from those in the past, she will be in bondage to the transference.

Transference also occurs when a survivor unconsciously expects a significant person in her present life to satisfy all her unfulfilled parental longings as a child. When that individual fails to live up to this fantasized role, the survivor may express emotions which reflect her feelings towards the failures of her real parents.

Anyone functioning as a support person to a multiple can expect some kind of transference to occur within the relationship. Therefore, when you can't logically understand a survivor's actions or reactions to you, consider this possibility. She may be unconsciously responding as if you were her childhood perpetrator, her non-protecting parent, or the idealized parent she never had.

Once the transference dynamic is recognized, it gives the problem a whole new perspective. Not only may it clarify what is occurring, but it can also provide a handle for addressing the pertinent childhood issue within the survivor from which it arises. Be prepared, however, for the possibility that the survivor may not recognize or accept the link between the past and the present as quickly as you do. Even if she is reluctant to acknowledge it, however, *your* increased insight will perhaps enable you to respond to her with greater patience and understanding while maintaining your own healthy boundaries with her.

Another important dynamic to be aware of when transference occurs in a relationship is the possibility that you could respond to it in a way that reflects *your own* unresolved issues from the past. This is called "counter-transference." When your emotional reactions get entangled with the survivor's, it can be harmful to her and disastrous to your relationship. The healthiest option in such a case is to withdraw from each other while you both address your own issues. Ask God to help you do this in a sensitive manner.

Their Appropriateness

Because of the powerful messages and conditioning abuse survivors received as children, they are generally quite confused about the appropriateness of their emotions. Being shamed or punished for showing an emotional response to abuse implants a message deep within a child's mind that such emotions are unacceptable.

Children groomed to participate in rituals or the production of child pornography are often deliberately conditioned to reflect no emotional reaction at all, regardless of what they experience. Such children are taught that control over their emotions is a virtue or an indicator of strength. Once established, these false beliefs will be carried into adulthood and continue to hinder the survivor's emotional healing unless they are traced to their origin and specifically countered with truth.

Those who believe that they are not supposed to have emotions need to learn that emotions are a normal and healthy part of everyone's life. If they were scolded or punished for their emotions, they need to learn that emotions are completely amoral. They can never be judged as good or bad, right or wrong. Sometimes what people choose to *do* with their emotions can be wrong but not the feelings themselves. Emotions are natural human responses to life's events. Their existence is as normal—and as uncontrollable—as hiccups, yawns, and sneezes.

Survivors who were taught that stifling emotions is the strong, mature way to handle them need to learn that emotions represent powerful energy. If that energy is not released in a healthy manner, it will affect the person in many indirect ways. In addition to causing psychosomatic physical ailments, repressed emotional energy can lead to depression, irritability, and other mental and emotional effects. When the barriers holding it back eventually begin to weaken, the uncharacteristic and inappropriate outbursts of anger which the person experiences can be damaging to important social relationships as well.

Learning truth on a cognitive level is rarely sufficient to change beliefs established in terrifying situations. As I explain in the next section, those beliefs must be addressed in the emotional context in which they were acquired.

Even after the belief is changed at this deep level, breaking the old behavior patterns can be a fearful proposition for survivors. Success will come only as they dare to do so and then experience no adverse effects.

As part of the survivor's support system, you can play an important role in this process by encouraging her in the right direction whenever you sense her stifling or otherwise struggling with the validity of her emotions. Repeatedly giving her permission to feel, own, and verbalize her emotions and then validating whatever emotions she does express will help her feel that her emotions really are legitimate. The more she hears and experiences your permission and validation, the more bold and successful she will be in overcoming her unhealthy patterns.

The following is an excellent example of how a therapist responded to his client's reluctance to allow the expression of the "stupid, blubbery emotions" of her child alters who had revealed some very traumatic memories:

> Do you want a reason for their blubbering and being all upset? You've been terribly, terribly hurt and you weren't allowed to react to it. You had terrible things done to you—terrible pain done to you—and yet in the midst of it you had to be controlled, you had to be perfect, you had to be still, and you had to do something with all the scared and hurt feelings, didn't you? You had to put those feelings away and now you have this big pool of feeling, a big pool of hurt. . . from years and years of having to be stuffed down, stuffed down, stuffed down, don't feel,

don't feel, don't feel.... Do you think that the little girl that had that electrode stuck on her chest and was shocked didn't hurt like mad? She deserves to know that her feelings are being validated by us too. She hurt terribly. It was scary. It was frightening. It was confusing.... Yet you knew that if you reacted back then, it would just make it worse. And you found a way to get through that without expressing any hurt. It doesn't mean that it wasn't there. It's there. It's very real and it's very deep. And that little girl needs to be able to express her hurt. The five year old [male alter] that was urinated on needs to be allowed to express how humiliated he felt. They couldn't cry back then. But it's okay to feel it now. I'm going to be here with you to get through it. Just let it out. You deserve to let it out. It's okay to start to feel the real feelings again.[2]

A therapist is, of course, supposed to be able to handle the full force of a survivor's emotions. Your capacity may not necessarily be as great. Evaluating this upfront and establishing your own boundaries is wise. You need to consider your own emotional health and the effect that another's pain or anger might have on your own "unfinished business." Taking care of yourself and not entering a role in which you cannot perform well is the healthiest route for you to take, for both yourself and the survivor.

Processing Memories

The true goal of therapy is not just for the survivor to learn how to express her emotions, however. Rather it is to bring healing to the underlying sources of pain. This requires accessing the traumatic memories in which the emotions are rooted and processing those events in a manner which seeks to eliminate the ongoing pain.

While physical pain was a very real part of the original trauma, the predominant ongoing pain is usually emotional in nature and is based on the *message(s)* which the child carried away from the event. Because children inherently lack mature cognitive skills, they are exceptionally prone to misinterpret what occurred and why. They often end up blaming themselves and judging their worth and value as a person in tremendously inaccurate ways.

For ritual abuse survivors these misconceptions are compounded by the fact that cultists often deliberately distorted their perception of reality through the use of drugs, sensory overload, sleep deprivation, hypnosis, and other illusionary tactics. These perpetrators are keenly aware of the importance of beliefs in shaping behavior. They therefore deliberately structured events to manipulate the survivor's beliefs in order to instill a sense of powerlessness and control by the cult.

The end result is that many beliefs that children carry away from their traumatic experiences are simply not true. This is unfortunate because of the years of unnecessary pain those false beliefs perpetuate in their lives. The silver lining to this dark cloud, however, is that even though the traumatic events cannot be undone, the memories can be revisited and the erroneous messages they spawned in the child corrected to reflect truth. When this occurs, the pain associated with them is instantly dispelled.

The other encouraging factor is that facilitating this kind of healing does not necessarily take a skilled therapist. Supporters who are willing to learn the basic procedure can often be extremely effective in this kind of ministry. They will also find that it works just as well with non-multiples.

The steps involved are quite simple but very important for keeping the process on track. Memory work is never pleasant, but by focusing on a specific goal, the intensified pain evoked in the survivor will be not only productive, but also confined to a minimum length of time.

The first step is to trace the particular pain (or fear, belief, compulsion, or behavioral tendency) that the survivor is feeling back to its origin. Starting with what the survivor is already in touch with is most efficient because the door to the memory from which it comes is already open. You just have to ask her to drift back in her mind to when she first felt this pain or ask Jesus to take her to the memory. If He believes she is ready to encounter it, He may put her instantly in touch with it.

Sometimes neither of these methods will successfully connect the survivor with the originating memory. Unfortunately the many other dynamics operating in a multiple's life can interfere with the process. Some involve the survivor herself while others were imposed upon her system by external sources. Internal protector alters who are invested in keeping the survivor functional may block access to the memory if they think she would be too overwhelmed by it. Sometimes other psychological conflicts around the issue of "knowing" need to be resolved before the mind will release the memory. At other times programming or demonization may be involved in causing the block. While you may be able to remove demonic blocks through spiritual warfare, addressing programming or conflict issues may require a therapist's attention.

When contact with the traumatic memory is successful, however, the next step is to identify the message(s) causing the pain (or other troubling symptoms). You can help the survivor pinpoint this by asking what this event caused her to believe about herself, others, or life in general or what decisions she made as a result of it. Be sure she understands that the beliefs you are searching for must come out of her emotional state at the time of the event, which might be totally different from what her adult mind tells her is true.

While each survivor must identify these messages for herself in each situation, some of the common beliefs which children carry away from abusive events are:

It was my fault.
I am bad.
I am dirty, contaminated.
I am unlovable.
I don't matter.
My body is not my own.
I am possessed by my perpetrator.
I am powerless to protect myself.
I am powerless to change anything.

Usually the beliefs giving rise to the greatest pain focus on the person's identity, worth, or destiny in life.

When the specific message causing the pain is identified, the survivor's anguish will usually increase. While this is uncomfortable, healing is most effective when she is actively embracing the full impact of the believed message as you embark upon the next step, which is to challenge its accuracy.

One powerful way of doing this, if you and the survivor are both comfortable with it, is to invite Jesus to address the truthfulness of the belief. While you must never assume that He will answer "on demand," He will frequently choose to intervene in some way that clearly impresses upon the survivor or alter what the TRUTH really is. When this occurs, both the false belief and the pain derived from it instantly evaporate. Peace and calm replace the often gut-wrenching agony previously experienced.[3]

This method for healing emotional pain is based on John 8:32, where Jesus said, "You shall know the truth, and the truth shall set you free." Because God is the author of all truth, the same measure of healing can result regardless of the means by which the truth is received.

Sometimes in the course of revisiting a memory, the deliberate manipulations of the cult to deceive the survivor will become clear, and this *truth* will successfully banish her false beliefs based upon it. At other times an alter's beliefs about a particular situation can be totally revolutionized by having another alter supply a piece of *truth* which was previously missing because of the dissociative barriers, and this will instantly dispel a lie message. Reading carefully chosen portions of Scripture may also be effective in bringing *truth* if it addresses the specific false belief causing the survivor's pain.

While healing truth can be received from any source which the survivor accepts as an authority, you yourself may fall short in ascertaining the exact piece of truth needed to dispel a particular false belief. When that happens, you will not see the dramatic healing described above. Jesus is the only One who consistently knows what particular truth the survivor needs in each situation. That is why He is the best one to supply the truth. While the possibility of deception from demons or other alters certainly exists when seeking truth from God, what is not truth will be immediately known because it will fail to have a healing effect on the survivor.

Sometimes the emotional pain being felt by the survivor is connected to a series of memories linked together by a common false belief. Complete healing seemingly requires that she be in touch with the memory of the event at which that belief was *first* established. When Jesus does not respond to your request to bring *truth* or the healing does not seem complete, it may be due to the fact that the survivor is not yet in touch with that critical initial memory. In this case you can ask Jesus to continue leading her back further and further until she reaches it.

When *truth* is received and the pain is removed from a memory, it may no longer be considered intolerable. This may lead to further steps of healing as the dissociative barriers which have isolated it for so many years may no longer be needed.

Anger

In addition to overwhelming pain, abuse also generates considerable anger. While the pain is often based on false beliefs, the anger is usually fully justified. It is the body's natural response to a wrong suffered. Because it was usually not safe or permissible for survivors to express their anger at the time of the abuse, it becomes a significant issue to be addressed in their healing process.

Resolving anger begins in a manner similar to pain in that it needs to be connected to a specific incident or issue. Because of the dissociation and many intervening years, the specific source of the anger is not always obvious to the survivor at first. Nevertheless the best starting place is to ask her precisely who she is angry at and why.

If she reports that her anger stems from a recent event, but its intensity seems excessive, its extra force is probably coming from a similar, but more serious, incident in her past. You can probe for this deeper source by asking if she remembers feeling this kind of anger before or if she sees anything about the issue inciting her current anger that reminds her of her past abuse.

Once she connects her anger to its true root, she needs to ascertain its validity. Was she truly wronged, or is her anger based on an inaccurate perception of the event? Help her process the memory as described above to rectify any erroneous beliefs associated with it. Anger which was rooted in a false belief will instantly dissolve when the belief is corrected.

If her anger is based on an accurate assessment of the original event and she truly was wronged, she needs a safe way to express her anger so its energy can be dissipated and no longer be triggered in response to current events or affect her health psychosomatically. Several options can provide this necessary release. She can use the Gestalt technique of imagining her perpetrator sitting in a chair in front of her and vocalizing the full extent of her anger as if to his or her true presence. In the Bible, David often vehemently expressed his anger directly to God, and the survivor can do this as well if she chooses. Sometimes engaging in a forceful physical activity while verbalizing one's anger helps to dissipate more of its energy. In this case she can beat a chair cushion with her fist or a tennis racket, or she can whack a counter or the back of a chair with a rolled up newspaper.

These more physical means of releasing anger are especially necessary when the strength of the anger being felt might lead the survivor to some form of violence. Anger of this potency is not unusual in survivors of horrendous abuse. In such a situation she may need to initiate the controlled physical action even before analyzing the exact nature and source of her anger. You can then help guide her thinking in this direction as she is engaged in the physical activity or after its energy is reduced to a more manageable level.

Forgiveness is another key component of dealing with anger, but the rlationship between the two dynamics is often confusing. **Anger** is a *feeling*. Therefore its *existence* is not under the control of the will. It is the body's *natural response* to a wrong suffered. It is not condemned by God unless it is acted out in a harmful way or retained too long (Eph. 4:26). **Hate** is often closely associated with anger, perhaps fueled by it. It must not be confused with anger, however. **Hate** is not a feeling, but a *chosen attitude* which desires revenge or wishes ill on another person.

Forgiveness is an *act of the will* by which we mentally release our perpetrator(s) from their "debt" to us (Luke 11:4), that is, the penalty which justice demands for their wrong-doing. We relinquish all demands for retribution and desires for revenge to God's higher tribunal of justice (Rom. 12:19; Col. 3:25; Gen. 18:25). **Forgiveness** thus surrenders the *hate* in our heart towards our abuser. Forgiveness is actually a gift from God by which we can regain emotional health in spite of being grievously wronged.

Although it is commanded by God (Mark 11:25), forgiveness does not occur naturally or instantly. The truth is that in order to fully forgive, one must fully comprehend the nature and implications of the wrong suffered. While this soaks in, anger is a natural and expected emotional response. In fact, if the survivor feels no anger as she processes a horribly abusive memory, she is still dissociating the anger. She cannot be fully healed until she is willing to own the anger and address it through healthy channels.

Many people believe that forgiveness should automatically eliminate your anger towards the offender. They fail to recognize that anger is a natural emotion, which cannot be affected by an act of the will. Its energy may or may not be adequately dissipated when forgiveness is granted.

The survivor must fully understand this so that she will address any remaining anger in a healthy manner and not try to deny its existence by stifling it or turning it inward on herself. She can still be legitimately angry about what her perpetrators did, how they did it, why they did it, why it hurt so deeply, how unfair it was, and the effects that it is having *without demanding revenge*. This kind of anger is especially understandable when memories are fresh.

Holding onto this anger for any significant amount of time will be detrimental to the survivor's health physically, emotionally, and spiritually, however. Therefore she must continue to process the offense until she can come to terms with it and put it to rest. Sometimes additional rehashing of the event and its various ramifications will enable her to do this. If the anger is particularly strong, she may need to ventilate it in a more physical way so its energy gets depleted and she can be free of its effects in her life.

The complicating dynamics of DID must also be kept in mind when dealing with the survivor's anger. As long as dissociation is in place, the alters must be recognized as having their own separate part of the survivor's mind, will, and emotions. Therefore, just because one part has resolved its anger and forgiveness issues does not mean that they all have.

You should also expect anger, hate, and forgiveness to wax and wane throughout the therapeutic journey as new memories and issues continually arise. Each wave of new awareness of the brutality the survivor suffered will naturally be accompanied by anger and perhaps temporarily renewed desires for revenge.

Guilt

Most ritual abuse survivors were not only incredibly traumatized themselves but were also forced to traumatize others. If their cult involvement was extensive, they probably even participated in human sacrifices and other criminal acts. Furthermore, if they had younger siblings or even children of their own who were under the age of 6 and able to dissociate, their cult-involved alters were possibly forced to bring them into cult activities as well.

Such acts of perpetration were usually totally contrary to both the will and moral standards of the Core and Host personalities. They could only be tolerated through extreme dissociation. The protective walls concealing these memories will therefore be exceptionally strong. Sooner or later, however, in order for healing to be complete, the survivor will have to face and own these unbearable realities.

As these memories come into her consciousness, she may be overcome by intense feelings of guilt. When those victimized by her actions were her own children, she may feel totally incapable of handling the implications. Her vehement self-blame may potentially lead her to serious acts of self-punishment or thoughts of suicide.

This is one of the most critical times for her to have the support of other caring individuals who can understand and affirm the nature of her emotional response but also provide a degree of objectivity. The main goal in addressing her enormous feelings of guilt is to help her discern where true responsibility for the evil acts lies. She is *NOT* responsible for actions she was forced—or manipulated—into performing. The one *forcing* the action bears the guilt (Mark 9:42).

In cases of ritual sacrifices and murder, a particularly powerful message to convey to the survivor is that she was as innocent as the knife. She was used and had absolutely no choice in the matter. Her alter-personalities were exploited and maneuvered by intense, terror-filled double binds to perform as virtual robots. Sometimes these memories may need to be repeatedly rehearsed until this truth is clearly evident and grasped. This is also a very appropriate time to ask Jesus to address the beliefs which underlie her painful emotions.

As memories become clearer, you can also sometimes help the survivor recognize how guilt was purposely used to manipulate and control her. Perpetrators often force an alter to commit some kind of crime just so they can use it as blackmail to secure the alter's silence and the tight cover-up needed for their covert criminal activities. They can get significant cooperation by holding over the child's head the threat that "If you tell what *we* did, we'll tell what *you* did—and you'll go to jail!" Sometimes these extreme guilt-provoking acts were forced upon the survivor because of the intense emotional conflict it would create, thus producing the strong dissociative barriers which would protect the Core and Host from knowledge of the event and effectively hide the activities the cultists desired to keep secret.

Fear

By far the most powerful emotion used for manipulation by cults, however, is fear. This is the driving force behind all their mechanisms of control. Cult victims were repeatedly subjected to terrifying and life-threatening double binds in which the only way out was to comply with the wishes of the perpetrator(s). By means of this cruel treatment they could essentially force the survivor into any desired behavior.

The end result is that whenever these survivors encounter something which in any way resembles a part of those terrifying situations, their subconscious minds automatically associate it with those previous events, and they instantly respond with the same adrenaline-pumping fear. They may not even be consciously aware of the memories, but their emotions respond just the same.

Virtually anything associated with the survivors' perpetrator(s), the cult, or their abuse, whether deliberately used or randomly present, can trigger a flashback reaction of fear and panic when encountered at a later time. These triggers may include specific types of animals, birds, insects, objects, or symbols. Survivors may also be sensitized to certain activities associated with the cult, such as sitting in circles or around bonfires, chanting, or swaying to music as well as to various locations used for cult gatherings, such as woods, barns, mines, or caves. Even weather conditions which occurred during the abuse or behaviors which evoked strong punishment, such as saying "No," doing it wrong, or performing imperfectly can evoke an inner terror for the survivor. Encountering any of these triggers frequently provokes a switch in personalities, often to the victim alter most directly related to the fear or a protector alter who believes the survivor is in imminent danger.

Understanding why these fears exist and why they are so powerful, so tenacious, and often so seemingly irrational is critical to the role of a support person. Discounting them or expecting them to be quickly resolved will be counterproductive. As you learn the particular things which trigger the survivor you are supporting grows, you can be alert for them and, when possible, even protect her from unnecessary exposure to what may cause an uncomfortable reaction in her.

Because these fears are associated with survival threatening situations, they are extremely difficult to erase. If the memories in which they are rooted have not yet surfaced, working on overcoming them is virtually impossible. Even after the memories are reached, desensitizing the triggers will take time. You may choose to be less protective in guarding the survivor from exposure to them, but consult with her therapist before deliberately confronting her with a known trigger for the purpose of desensitization.

When she does encounter these triggers and her fears erupt, continue treating her with gentleness, patience, comfort, and reassurance.

Help her notice the differences between the current setting and the past terror-evoking events, especially the things which may indicate her safety in the present situation.

Keep in mind, too, that fears can sometimes be demonically driven, in which case spiritual warfare is the proper antidote. Fear in itself can also be a foothold which empowers demonic activity. Encouraging the survivor to deal with her fears is therefore important. It can never be forced, however. She must be personally motivated and willing to cooperate in the effort.

Processing Current Life Experiences

In addition to processing the traumatic events of their past, SRA survivors often need to talk about things which are transpiring in their current lives. The dynamics of dissociation and programming, as well as the emotionally upsetting nature of the therapy process, make everyday life a little more complicated and challenging for multiples. Emotions and frustrations often mount and need a chance to be ventilated. You can be a great help by lending a listening ear, providing an objective perspective, and at times offering some good advice.

One area that is tremendously affected by the survivor's multiplicity issues is inter-personal relationships. Perhaps those most complex involve her family of origin. To what extent they believe and support the survivor can vary greatly and have an immense impact on her. If they happen to be her perpetrators, these relationships carry a ton of potent, and often conflicting, emotions. Ongoing or sporadic contact with *any* former perpetrator can be extremely upsetting. These are all situations in which the survivor needs wise and compassionate support.

If the survivor also has a family acquired through marriage, these relationships are majorly affected by her multiplicity issues as well. She may carry a tremendous amount of grief over the difficulties she knows she is causing for those she loves the most. If she is able to work, that is another setting where special challenges may occur. Being able to talk to another caring individual about these things can be very helpful and also enables therapy time to focus on issues that really do require a therapist.

One of the key elements which talking to another person provides is perspective. Because a multiple's life experience and memory are divided through dissociation, perspective often gets distorted. If alter-personalities lack a complete picture of a given situation, they can easily jump to wrong conclusions and go through unnecessary emotional reactions. Sometimes another person with a more objective perspective can turn a mountain into a mole hill rather quickly.

This isn't always true, however. Sometimes alters can be extremely convinced that their perspective is absolutely right! In these cases the combined input of several other people agreeing on a particular point of view may be necessary to convince an alter that she isn't seeing the whole picture.

Survivors also need help with perspective in recognizing when they overreact to things in the present because of their unresolved issues from the past. Whether it is buried anger that is "piggy-backing" on a current situation in order to vent some stored up energy or transference distorting their viewpoint, survivors often have a difficult time recognizing when these dynamics occur. Therefore an objective and supportive person can not only be instrumental in providing this perspective, but also help process the emotions that are aroused.

Physical Support

While providing emotional support to a survivor is best done in person, it can at times be ministered just as well over the phone or even at times by e-mail. Other needs, however, definitely require the supporter's physical presence. For lack of a better word, I am calling this kind of ministry "physical support."

Protection from Self-Harm

The most critical time this is needed is when the survivor's physical safety is in jeopardy. Unfortunately, self-harm and suicidal tendencies are quite common among this particular population. All threats of suicide need to be taken seriously. However, the unique dynamics of DID must also be kept in mind. Rarely does the whole system want to die. Other alters who are highly committed to life will often counterbalance the drive for death. They may spontaneously work to maintain the safety of the system or can be called upon to do so. Furthermore, the issue driving the suicidal urge, when identified, can often be quickly resolved. Frequently the alter desiring death does not have a complete or accurate picture of reality.

Self-harm can take many forms, including cutting, clawing, burning, bruising, and even fracturing bones of the body. The mechanisms driving this behavior can be quite complex. Frequently injurious behavior is connected to programming or demonization, but it can involve human dynamics as well.

Cult perpetrators usually use some form of mind control programming to keep their subjects under their strict control and serving their purposes. This sophisticated form of conditioning places a child in a terrifying double bind in which the desired response is seen as the only way out. By repeatedly attaching a specific "trigger" to this event, encountering the trigger alone will eventually compel the same response. Through this mechanism perpetrators can compel an almost automatic response of self-harm or suicide if strictly prohibited behaviors occur, such as any breach of secrecy or disobedience to major cult directives.

Sacrifice of oneself to Satan or some other supposed deity is also often expected in Satanic cults. Even unwilling alters can be manipulated into making such vows under extreme duress. Often a specific date is set, perhaps decades in advance, and programming put in place to ensure the carrying out of this commitment.

Demons can play a significant role in causing self-harm and suicide as well. Just as in the biblical account of the demonized man of the Gadarenes, who cut himself with stones (Mark 5:5), demonized alters may engage in similar acts of self-mutilation, especially when they are provoked.

Since demonic torment is an excellent way to enhance compliance, alters are frequently manipulated to establish a legal ground for demonic attachments. These demons can seemingly be given specific assignments that serve to enhance programming or ensure that the vows, oaths, and commitments the person made in the cult are indeed fulfilled.

Personal experience also indicates that demons may view being expelled from a person without accomplishing their assignments as demoralizing. Therefore, if deliverance seems imminent or progress in therapy in any way threatens the success of their mission, they may attempt to drive the survivor to commit suicide. From their perspective the survivor's suicide will spare them the horrible disgrace of being expelled in complete failure. While they cannot superimpose their will over the will of a Christian survivor, they are capable of injecting compulsive, morbid thoughts and/or inflicting tremendous psychic torment within the survivor's mind, which can sometimes impel the drastic response they desire.

Even apart from programming and demonization, however, alter-personalities known as "persecutors" may use self-harm to punish other alters whom they believe are not performing properly. These alters either were manipulated and brainwashed to take on the agenda of the perpetrators or surmised early in their existence that identifying with them was the safest route to go. They therefore virtually serve as internal representatives of the abuser(s) and instigate punishment whenever they perceive another alter's plans or actions to be displeasing to the external abuser.

As strange as it may sound, some protector alters may also cut or hurt the body when they feel the person is misperforming in the eyes of the perpetrator. In this case they are trying to warn the person that they are in danger of much more serious repercussions from the perpetrators if they do not amend their ways. Only a multiple can understand how effectively dissociation enables them to view the body that gets hurt as not being their own.

For other alters self-harm serves as a silent release for powerful emotions which they believe can be discharged in no other way. Still others use it as a coping strategy, endeavoring to convert intense emotional pain into physical pain, which to them seems more bearable.

Some people believe that subjecting the body to trauma is a means of strengthening the dissociative walls which protect the Core and the Host from knowing the truth about the evil that has been forced upon them. Therefore, if something occurs which threatens this desired separation, some part of the system may deliberately subject the body to retraumatization in an effort to strengthen the dissociative barriers protecting the Core and Host from the trauma-bearing parts of the system.[4]

This may occur, for example, if overwhelming memories surface, endangering secrets are revealed, incriminating knowledge is received, or a past perpetrator re-enters the survivor's life. Because of this dynamic whenever self-harm occurs, exploring whether the system is feeling a new threat of some kind is a wise step. Often addressing this issue will defuse the perceived need for further harm.

When the issues driving the self-harm or suicidal ideation cannot be quickly resolved, survivors may need around-the-clock surveillance to ensure their safety until whatever is precipitating the crisis can be resolved. Hospitalization is sometimes an option for providing this.

However, the survivor must have insurance—or significant financial resources. In addition, the hospital ideally needs to have staff trained to recognize and address both the psychological and spiritual dynamics operating within SRA survivors, which is rarely the case. Many psychiatric hospitals even refuse to recognize the reality of DID and/or SRA. Treatment in such a hospital will not be in the survivor's best interests and may even feel abusive.

In the absence of suitable hospitalization, a support person or a team of volunteers working in rotating shifts may need to provide the necessary surveillance. These people must be capable of physically, but non-abusively, restraining the survivor when necessary. Also, the more familiar they are with the dynamics of DID, conflict resolution, spiritual warfare, and the alter system of the survivor, the better equipped they will be to work with the survivor in a manner which diminishes, rather than enhances, the dynamics driving the crisis.

Sometimes a similar period of "constant companionship" may be needed to protect the survivor from physical access by the cult as well. In either situation be careful in choosing the location for such heightened surveillance so that small children are not exposed to potential violence or demonic confrontation. The need for this degree of physical protection varies greatly from survivor to survivor—and from month-to-month, week-to-week, or even day-to-day.

Assistance with Daily Living

Functionality among multiples also varies greatly. Some are super-achievers maintaining high level jobs while others are significantly disabled. Most will find, however, that functionality decreases somewhat as therapy intensifies. The saying that it sometimes "gets worse before it gets better" generally applies when dealing with childhood abuse issues. Therapy can often be paced, however, to minimize such a decrease in functionality. Therefore if you, as a supporter, see this occurring, you may want to report it to the therapist, who can possibly slow things down a little to prevent overwhelming and incapacitating the client.

Depending on the survivor's level of functionality, your physical presence may occasionally be needed to help with certain essential tasks of life, especially when a supportive spouse is not in the picture. If the survivor's system is particularly unstable for any reason, she may need assistance with such things as shopping, paying bills, or keeping various appointments. Frequent switching can disrupt the consistency needed to carry out these tasks.

Visits to the doctor can be a particularly stressful challenge for survivors, often precipitating instability and switching. This is not only confusing to the doctor and embarrassing to the survivor, but it can also hinder important communication between them. Child alters can be especially frightened of doctors' visits and may need comfort and reassurance that no abuse will occur. Having a knowledgeable person accompany the survivor on these occasions to provide this input and support, as well as assure adequate communication, is often helpful.

If parts of the survivor's system interfere with her ability to get to therapy appointments on time, having someone to drive her there may be beneficial. At other times her emotional state may render her unable or unsafe to drive, and she will appreciate having volunteers temporarily provide transportation for her.

Being too overwhelmed emotionally to function adequately is not uncommon for survivors from time to time. If they have small children at home, they may welcome somebody taking care of the children for a few hours so they can have some time alone to process new information, work with their alter system, or just try to "pull things together." This can be especially helpful immediately following therapy sessions.

Whatever type of physical support you give, be careful not to overreact or baby the survivor. Allow her to be as responsible as possible for her own needs with as much freedom as seems safe. Overdoing in this area of support can contribute to keeping her in a dependent state, which is counterproductive to her healing.

Spiritual Support

Ritual abuse survivors are held in bondage by spiritual forces of evil in addition to the deep psychological issues arising from their severe trauma. Therefore they will never achieve complete healing through human resources alone. God is the only One having the power and authority to overcome the forces of Satan ensnaring their souls—and He will do it in response to the prayers and spiritual warfare of His people. Assisting survivors in freeing themselves from their bondage to Satan and strengthening their relationship to God are therefore valuable areas of support which all survivors can use.

Prayer

While spiritual support can involve other aspects as well, a prayer focus will always be primary. Prayer unlocks the door to the outpouring of God's power, wisdom, and guidance for both you and the survivor. It is not only vital for achieving her healing but is crucial for addressing your inadequacies as well. While you may frequently feel at a complete loss in knowing how to help the survivor, God perfectly understands the issues and dynamics operating in her life. He also has the power to intervene, either acting directly in the survivor's life or guiding you in meeting the need. Your weakness is merely an opportunity for God to release His resources in you (2 Cor. 3:4-5; 12:9-10).

The powerful resource of prayer can be implemented without necessarily having direct contact with the survivor if that is inconvenient or uncomfortable. However, you obviously can pray most knowledgeably when you have some means of staying current with specific and ongoing needs. If several individuals are involved in providing spiritual support for a survivor, a prayer chain solely for this purpose can be an effective way to convey requests in a timely manner. Of course, confidentiality is of utmost importance.

Some of the general needs for which a ritual abuse survivor needs prayer include:
- Success in breaking through and eliminating all aspects of programming
- Success in recognizing and eliminating demonic footholds
- Discernment of truth from deception wherever Satan is involved
- Strength and courage to face and own the truth
- Guidance for the therapist
- Spiritual protection for the survivor and those helping her
- Adequate social and emotional support for her and her family
- Adequate finances and provisions for daily living needs

God is so gracious and loving toward His children that even when you don't know exactly how to pray for a survivor in a particular situation, you can just lift her name before His throne and know that the Holy Spirit will intercede on her behalf with "groans which words cannot express" (Rom. 8:26). How awesome it is to know that God's response does not depend on our ability to articulate the right words!

Spiritual Warfare

Because of the extensive demonization that occurs in SRA, anyone providing support for this kind of survivor needs a good understanding of the principles of spiritual warfare and the ability to engage effectively in it. Some may be particularly gifted in assisting in this manner and can play an invaluable role in helping the survivor gain lasting freedom from the forces of darkness she was usually forced to receive against her will. Others can assist in binding demons which attempt to interfere with her day-to-day life.

You must not enter this role without adequate preparation, however. Satan's forces can easily overpower an unprotected human, especially if you start "stepping on their toes." As a Christian, you may not be physically assaulted like the seven sons of Sceva were in the days of the Apostles (Acts 19:13-16), but you could suffer other severe blows to your well-being. Satan has the ability to manipulate circumstances around you, attack your health, or subtly work to cause moral deterioration in your life (cf. Job; Luke 13:11; 2 Cor. 11:3; 1 Tim. 4:1). This should not be threatening to a mature Christian, however, because God is infinitely more powerful than Satan (1 John 4:4), and He has provided all we need to be completely protected from his crafty schemes (Eph. 6:10-13).

Because Satan is a *spiritual* being and the battle we wage against him occurs on a *spiritual* plane, we need *spiritual* armor as our protection. In Ephesians 6:14-17 God clearly explains what that armor entails. Each piece is extremely important, and "putting them on" must never be viewed as merely a daily ritual of verbally rehearsing the words of these verses. While such a daily reminder is helpful, it is *the manifestation of a lifestyle which consistently exhibits these qualities* which provides protection in the spiritual realm. Because this protective armor is so important, the last chapter in this book is devoted to explaining it in greater depth.

Equipping ourselves in this spiritual armor provides our *defense* in the spiritual battle and is totally *our* responsibility. To launch an *offensive* attack against the enemy, we must be equally well prepared, but in this case we must not rely on any resource of our own. Only the power and authority of God Himself can successfully defeat the powers of darkness, and we must never forget this.

God, however, graciously allows His born again children to share the same spiritual position of authority in the heavens that He gave to His own Son, Jesus Christ, far above all the ranks of Satan's forces (Eph. 1:20-22; 2:6). Jesus Christ rightly deserves this position through His own divine merit. We share it only through His grace. Therefore, while we can command the obedience of Satan's forces just like Jesus modeled for us during His time on earth, we must do it in the power and authority of *His* name and on the basis of *His* shed blood.

If you are not a true child of God through faith in Jesus' death on the Cross for the forgiveness of your sins (John 1:12; 3:16-18), you do not share His position of authority and can wield no power against Satan or any of his demons. To try to do so could be disastrous (see Acts 19:13-16). When you *are* truly God's child, however, you can confidently engage in spiritual warfare on behalf of yourself and others, including the survivor(s) you are supporting.

Launching an offensive attack against the spiritual realm of darkness involves authoritatively commanding demons *"in the name of Jesus"* to do exactly what you want or do not want them to do. Because Satanic cultists often create alters or incorporate demons within a survivor's alter-personality system with the name of "Jesus" or "God," using a more specific description which refers *only* to the *divine* Jesus is often helpful when working with SRA survivors. By using designations such as "Jesus of Nazareth," "the risen Lord Jesus Christ," or "Jesus, my Redeemer," you eliminate all opportunities for confusion and substitution within the system dynamics of the survivor and the spiritual realm.

Usually demons will respond immediately to such commands. If they do not, you need to take into consideration several potentially complicating factors. Always remember that demons operate very legalistically within a strict authority structure (Eph. 1:21; 6:12). In some situations you may need to address the demon(s) in higher authority over the one whose activity you are targeting. A good pattern to use in spiritual warfare is to address the demon responsible for the given activity "and all those above and below" this one.

The higher in rank a demon is, the more he may resist responding to your commands in the name of Jesus. Demons can employ a lot of stall tactics, but they must ultimately obey. Therefore be persistent in your efforts, and remember that it is not your insistence, your tone, or your volume which determines the demon's response. It is the *authority* of the Lord Jesus Christ. You do not need to raise your voice or get hyped up emotionally to make a demon obey. These fleshly tactics have no effect in the spiritual realm except to amuse and flatter the demons involved.

Instead, rely wholly on spiritual weapons in your offensive attack (2 Cor. 10:3-4). For instance, you can often "turn up the heat" on the enemy by reading from the Bible, speaking, or singing about the shed blood of Jesus through which He triumphed over Satan and his forces (Heb. 2:15; Col. 2:15). These powerful spiritual weapons seem to cause such torment to the demons that they will often comply immediately to make it stop. If they do not, however, don't prolong this tactic because the person or alter to whom the demon is attached feels the nearly unbearable torment as well.

Another factor to keep in mind is that demons do not have to leave if their presence is based on a legal foothold established in the person's life. In DID this could be a sacrifice, vow, or covenant which a particular alter made or an evil activity in which the survivor was forced to participate. Sometimes alters willingly receive demons because of the supernatural power they offer, thinking they will serve to protect them from further trauma. For this reason some alters may be reluctant to let go of them. Until these footholds are renounced by the specific alter involved, the demon(s) will not have to leave.

You can, however, still use the authority of Jesus to bind their activity (Mat. 16:19). Experience has shown, in fact, that you can be very specific in doing this, even commanding that they be made deaf, dumb, blind, and/or totally paralyzed. You can also at least temporarily cancel their assignment in the individual.

Sometimes in order to work effectively with the alter involved, you need to command the demon(s) to be separated from the human alter(s). This gives the alters the ability to think for themselves in deciding to break the ties they have to the demon(s).

In dealing with SRA survivors, some of the areas in which spiritual warfare is needed include:
- Removing spiritual blindness from the hearts and minds of alters who are in bondage to Satan
- Prohibiting demons from blocking truth or interfering with therapy
- Stopping demonically driven fear, anxiety, confusion, torment, or self-harm

- Stopping demonic communication between the survivor and other cult members
- Providing spiritual protection
  - Whenever contact with cult-involved family members is necessary or possible
  - During Satanic holidays when accessing is likely (See Appendix E for calendar dates.)

Some examples for addressing these issues are:
- In the name of Jesus Christ, my Redeemer, I bind the ability of all demons to hinder truth and healing in the therapy session today.
- In the name of Jesus Christ of Nazareth I command the demons who are tormenting (name) to stop. Your assignment is cancelled and you must obey the orders of Jesus instead.
- If demons are in any way contributing to the confusion (name) is feeling, I command in the name of the risen Lord Jesus Christ that you stop and that you become mute and frozen.

In praying for spiritual protection, you might pray along these lines:
- Lord Jesus, I ask that You surround (name) with Your holy angels as she travels to her grandmother's. I ask that you block all demonic communication which might emanate from her grandmother or any other cult person associated with her. Allow no physical, emotional, or spiritual harm to come to her.
- Heavenly Father, I pray in the name of Jesus Christ, my risen Redeemer, that You send Your angelic forces in sufficient strength and number to completely overpower all of Satan's forces which may attempt to interfere with the deliverance session scheduled for (name) today.
- Almighty Creator God, I pray in the precious and holy name of Jesus Christ, my Savior, that You put an impenetrable hedge of spiritual protection around (name) through this

Satanic holiday so that all efforts by the cult to contact her will be blocked.

Sometimes Christian therapists allow, or even encourage, support people to accompany survivors during therapy sessions. This not only enables supporters to follow-up with the survivors much more knowledgeably after the session, but also gives them the opportunity to provide emotional and spiritual support *during* the session. In this way they can engage in spiritual warfare exactly as it is needed during this critical time. This is extremely valuable as Satan's greatest efforts to hinder the release of the survivors are often unleashed in the therapy session.

Specific spiritual warfare needs arising during the therapy session may include:

- Binding the ability of demons to hear and respond in any harmful way
- Binding the ability of demons to block truth and healing
- Binding demons which prohibit alters from speaking
- Binding demonic guards blocking access to significant memories or alters
- Binding demons who may hinder alters from hearing God's voice of truth
- Unmasking deceptive demonic imagery
- Binding demons from interfering as alters remember and renounce the legal grounds which provide the demonic attachment(s) (oaths, vows, covenants, sacrifices, etc.)
- Casting out demons once their legal grounds are renounced

Your willingness to support a survivor in spiritual warfare will reap significant benefits for yourself as well as the survivor. You will undoubtedly grow in your understanding of the spiritual realm and will have the opportunity to apply your knowledge of spiritual warfare in a perhaps unprecedented way. You will also share the joyous rewards of seeing the power of God free the survivor from Satan's grip and then observing the changes that occur in her life as a result.

Bible Study and Discipleship

Another aspect of spiritual support involves instructing and strengthening survivors and their alters in the truths of God's Word. This is especially crucial for alters who have been demonized and/or extensively indoctrinated by the cult. If spiritual growth does not occur for alters after deliverance, demons may return and actually bring the survivor into greater bondage than before (Luke 11:24-26).

The cult works hard to impugn the character and trustworthiness of God in the minds of the alters with whom they work. Replacing these misrepresentations with truth from God's Word is essential both before and after cult-loyal alters put their faith in God. Sometimes false beliefs can be challenged by bringing them directly to God for assessment. Often He will impress the *truth* on the mind of the alter(s) in such a poignant way that it instantly eliminates all doubt.

When some of the survivor's alters are already grounded in spiritual truth, they can often spread truth internally to those alters who have renounced their allegiance to Satan and desire to follow God instead. Truth also spreads very naturally when alters are fused or integrated with spiritually mature parts of the system. Usually this rejoining is only successful, however, when marked differences of perspective are first eliminated. Therefore, a certain amount of instruction and discipleship may be necessary before it can occur.

Whether from God, other alters, or willing supporters; cult-indoctrinated alters need to understand and experience the *true* nature of God and learn the privileges of being His child. They need to discover and claim His many promises to them. They also need to learn the importance of faith and prayer as well as the elements of effective spiritual warfare so they can successfully defend themselves against Satan's efforts to bring them back under his bondage. In addition they need to learn the importance of ridding their lives of sin and filling it with the Holy Spirit.

When considerable demonization is present, discussion of spiritual issues can create significant disturbance in the system. Some survivors cannot even attend church because of the degree of internal torment and punishment they receive internally. Under these conditions spiritual instruction must be handled with great care, usually by a Christian therapist or well-trained pastor or layperson who will focus on the critical issues causing the resistance and impeding therapy. As counseling and deliverance progresses, internal opposition to spiritual truth will generally lessen, and the system will become more cooperative in allowing spiritual instruction from other sources as well.

Anyone contemplating a teaching role with a survivor must be alert to the potential problems and not enter this role unless they are prepared to deal with whatever opposition may arise. On rare occasions cult-loyal alters or demons may openly defy and even attack you.

Dealing with any kind of opposition requires the ability to discern between alters and demons. While demons will respond to spiritual warfare, alters will not. Defiant alters must be handled according to the conflict principles discussed in chapter 2. Treat them with a firm and cautious respect and don't try to force your own agenda. Refrain from doing or saying anything that would further ignite the system. If you are not experienced or confident in maneuvering such situations back to a productive conversation, try to withdraw from the enflaming topic. Be sure to report to the survivor's therapist the nature of the antagonism you encountered. Also be advised that many survivors experience little or no difficulties along this line.

Regardless of what the system will tolerate, discipleship often takes place best in the context of everyday life experiences. Short, succinct statements relevant to a current situation can catch the system off guard and have a profound effect on the alters who are present or listening. You may discover other creative means to expose parts of an otherwise resistant system to God's truth, such as strategically placed notes, cards, or plaques or the availability of Bible story books or coloring books for child alters. While you must always be sensitive to any evidence of opposition when doing these things, the survivor's system is usually much less apt to react to these unexpected and indirect bursts of spiritual education than to deliberately set up times for overt Bible study.

Financial Support

Many ritual abuse survivors need financial assistance at some point in their healing journey. Because treatment is a lengthy, and usually expensive, process, their financial resources frequently get depleted long before their healing is complete. Those who are unemployed and/or living on their own generally experience this need most critically, but others too may eventually need assistance in paying for therapy or even daily living necessities.

While you may not be able to meet this need entirely on your own, you can perhaps approach your church or share the need with an appropriate group that might be willing to contribute collectively to this need. You can also help the survivor connect to whatever social services may be available to help her make ends meet.

Remember that every good deed you do or every sacrifice you make stores up treasure for yourself in heaven (1 Tim. 6:18-19). Your generosity to others—whether of your time, your possessions, or your finances—opens the door for you to receive the same generosity in your time of need (Luke 6:38; Heb. 6:10). You never lose your reward for giving even a cup of cold water to one of God's needy children (Matt. 10:42).

Therapeutic Support

Professional counseling can cost $90 an hour or more. Even at reduced rates, the fee can be prohibitive to ritual abuse survivors without insurance or other significant financial resources. Furthermore, the number of professional counselors and psychologists knowledgeable of the unique dynamics involved in DID/SRA is currently insufficient to accommodate the ever-increasing number of ritual abuse victims seeking help. Those able to recognize and address the spiritual components involved are even fewer.

In light of these problems, alternative sources of therapy are needed. While it is not a totally ideal situation, certain lay individuals can be trained to do effective therapy with SRA survivors. Many who can secure help in no other way are eternally grateful for pastors and other willing laymen who have stepped in to help bridge the gap.

The truth is that most of the professionals working with this clientele obtained their knowledge of the unique dynamics of DID/SRA directly from the survivors themselves. While laymen may lack the broader psychological expertise of trained clinicians, they can also learn much directly from survivors. They can also tap into other resources that are available in the form of literature, seminars, and consultations with more experienced therapists. Because of the complexities involved in this diagnosis, a vast amount of networking occurs in this field with counselors sharing their own knowledge and experience with each other. Anyone eager to learn can get connected to this network quite easily.

Providing therapy for ritual abuse survivors is definitely not for everyone. Those considering this possibility must themselves be in reasonably good health—psychologically, emotionally, and spiritually—or their own unresolved issues will repeatedly interfere with their ability to do good therapy. Being disciplined in setting and maintaining good personal boundaries is extremely important. The very nature of DID requires that those who work with such clients be comfortable with handling all emotions and personality types as well as a wide range of sexual discussions. Skillfulness in interpersonal relationships is a must as well as commitment, sensitivity, love, and compassion.

This type of therapy is never easy. Those embarking upon it must be prepared for a long and challenging journey which will stretch them in many ways. It will also require a substantial investment of time, both in becoming educated and in working with the survivors. The opportunity to work in an apprentice type relationship with a more experienced clinician is the ideal way to learn the necessary skills involved but is not always possible.

If God lays it upon your heart to assume a therapeutic role with a survivor, He will guide you and sustain you through the process. Never assume such a role lightly, however, or without a definite calling from God.

Supporting Versus Caretaking

While ritual abuse survivors may appear to be extremely needy people, those desiring to help them recover from the painful tragedies in their lives must avoid falling into the trap of codependency. Feeling so sorry for them that you rush in to do everything possible to help them and to demonstrate your love for them is not necessarily the best approach. They certainly need good Christian love, but it must be given in a way that is truly beneficial and doesn't perpetuate their staying in a victim role. While this was obviously their position as children, a major goal of the treatment process is to bring them out of their victim mentality. This is why the term "survivor" is used so extensively with those who have suffered abuse.

The primary responsibility for recovery must always belong to the survivors. Taking on care which they can provide for themselves will be counter-productive in the long run. Also, do not try to become substitute "parents" for child alters. Instead, help them grieve what they did not receive as children in the way of adequate parenting and learn to care for themselves as adults.

Finally, take care of yourself to the same extent you care for the survivor. Because most abuse survivors are deficient in knowing correct boundary setting and self-care, your modeling these crucial dynamics will benefit them immensely.

None of these guidelines minimizes the need for genuine compassion and validation of the immense pain and difficult struggles which these survivors experience. Just don't be a rescuer—because that keeps them in a victim role. Although having someone else take care of them may *feel* so good and you may think that these survivors *deserve* it so much, it will not help them move towards greater health.

Therefore keep your focus on supporting in a way that empowers them rather than makes them more dependent on others for their needs.

The Role of the Church

The role the Church should play in supporting ritual abuse survivors is a controversial, yet crucial, question which must be addressed. If the Church truly functioned as the Body of Christ, survivors would find within its doors the same acceptance, compassion, nurture, and assistance that Jesus Christ Himself would give them.

Ideally the Church *seems like* the most logical place for these wounded individuals to find refuge, support, and spiritual instruction as they battle to free themselves from Satan's hold on their lives. In actual experience, however, ritual abuse survivors often discover that the Church has little understanding of the realities of DID, SRA, or demonization and is totally unprepared for dealing with them.

Unfortunately the underlying problems in the Church are not always easy to solve. Some are legitimate and understandable, stemming from a lack of knowledge or experience with this particular diagnosis. Others are more philosophical in nature, such as believing that SRA memories are really the result of an overly imaginative or fearful mind, that alter-personalities are really demons, or that Christians can't be demonized. Sadly, some stem from spiritual immaturity or a lack of godly obedience. Believers who are not well grounded in the Word are sometimes terrified of dealing with anything that has to do with Satan or demons. Others are unwilling to extend themselves beyond their own self-inscribed comfort zones.

The end result is that many ritual abuse survivors feel not only misunderstood but sometimes rejected, or even mistreated, by the Church. If this occurs repeatedly in church after church, they may eventually become totally disillusioned with the Church as an effective resource for their healing.

This is tragic for both the individual churches and the survivors and must certainly grieve God deeply. When a church fails to function as a true representation of God and His character to all those who enter its doors, it fails its responsibility to God and will one day be held accountable for this neglect. In addition, they miss the blessings and opportunities for growth that God perhaps intended them to receive through these wounded, but special, children of His.

It is tragic for survivors because all too often they interpret the failure of the Church as a failure of God's love for them. Feeling abandoned by both the Church and God, they may easily eliminate the most powerful resource they have for their healing.

The dramatic conversion of their cult-loyal alters may also be jeopardized. Often they were persuaded to make the mammoth decision of changing their allegiance from Satan to God because they were told that not only does God offer them forgiveness and freedom, but also that those in His kingdom operate with love and compassion. If they do not find that promised love and compassion in the Church, they may feel deceived or tricked, making God's kingdom no more appealing to them than Satan's realm.

While most survivors can accept that not everyone in a given church has the time, emotional capacity, and spiritual maturity to understand and reach out to them, they have difficulty grasping that *no one* can. Why should those with more "normal" needs be received more readily than they? Why should they feel rejected because they are too *unusual* or *extreme* in their needs? Jesus would not have turned His back on them. Why should His people?

The truth is that both SRA survivors and churches face a major dilemma when they confront each other. If the survivors have already had a bad experience in another church, they may struggle with whether to reveal their identity as a multiple with a history of ritual abuse to *this* church. If they do, they risk the possibility of further misunderstanding, conflict, and rejection with its accompanying pain.

On the other hand, if they choose to hide their identity and history from the church, they will have to remain very superficial in their relationships and will constantly feel that they are hiding a big secret about who they really are. In addition, they greatly decrease the possibility of getting any of their legitimate SRA-related needs met in the church. They will never know if perhaps some individuals in *this* church might truly be willing to embrace them for who they are and genuinely try to help them.

The church's dilemma is even more complex. First of all, having a known SRA survivor in the church generally forces the leadership to determine its philosophical position in regard to DID/SRA. This often entails facing and discussing issues which they never confronted before.

If they *are* willing to embrace the realities of DID and SRA, they face additional decisions regarding the nature and extent of their involvement in supporting the particular survivor(s) in their body. How far will they go beyond general love, acceptance, and prayer support? What are their resources in regard to time, personnel, and finances to devote in this direction? Where in priority does such a ministry fit?

Who will be involved in this ministry, and how will they be equipped for their role? Are they willing to spend time learning about DID and SRA? To what extent will they help with daily living needs if they arise? What about financial needs? Are they willing to create a special prayer chain for the survivor(s)'s needs? Will they be available in times of crisis?

If the church does not have an adequate counselor on staff, will they help the survivor(s) get good Christian therapy elsewhere? Is the pastor or another leader willing to interact with the survivor(s)'s therapist to enhance understanding and coordinate support or other interventions on behalf of the survivor(s)? Is the church willing to participate in deliverance, spiritual instruction, and discipleship for these individuals?

Finally, because of the controversial issues involved, the leaders must decide how open to be with the entire church body about its ministry to SRA survivors. Just because *they* have wrestled through the controversial issues involved doesn't mean that everyone in their ongregation has. They therefore need a measure of foresight regarding the particular problems which could arise in the body as a consequence of this ministry.

Unfortunately, the False Memory Syndrome Foundation has created considerable media hype challenging the accuracy of "recovered memories." Without being knowledgeable of the mechanism of dissociation and how the mind handles *traumatic* memories differently than ordinary memories, the general population has no sound basis on which to evaluate this issue.

Another closely related concern is the reliability of the allegations that SRA survivors make regarding the identity of cult perpetrators. These might potentially even be made towards other church members, producing a significant crisis for the church leaders.

The subject of demonization, with the fears and questions it raises, is another potentially divisive issue in the church. Many Christians would like to remain ignorant of this reality and may be especially hostile to anyone whom they perceive is "finding demons behind every bush." They may be totally convinced that Christian survivors cannot possibly "have demons." Others may err on the other side and insist that their entire problem is demonic, considering their alters to be demons.

At some point the amount of resources going towards such a small segment of the congregation may also seem inordinate. This could potentially cause problems too, especially if the church is small.

In light of all of these complicating factors, the most workable solution for supporting SRA survivors within a church seems to be through a team which maintains a low-profile in the church body. In this way neither the specialized ministry itself nor the issues it raises need interface with the entire congregation. It also allows survivors to have a small group of people with whom they can be "real" while at the same time being more protective of their identity and issues with the majority of the church.

Because supporting ritual abuse survivors can sometimes be demanding, time consuming, and draining, having a team enables the load to be spread among a number of individuals so that no one of them gets burned out. A team also enables supporters to serve in the area of their particular giftedness rather than being a "jack of all trades" to the survivor. If some are unable to become deeply involved emotionally, they can still be of assistance in providing things such as prayer support, discipleship, or transportation when needed.

Potential members of such a team can be judiciously selected by the church leaders. After being presented with the need and receiving a limited introduction and exposure to DID/SRA issues, this initial pool of hand-picked individuals can then decide whether to commit to actual participation on the team. Service must always be voluntary and on an "as able" basis.

Those who choose to be a part of this special ministry can then receive whatever further training is appropriate for their level of involvement (see Appendix C). While much of this may occur in an informal manner through contact with the survivor(s) involved, a more structured plan for educating and training a church support group for SRA survivors is presented in Appendix D.

Spiritual Protection

Whenever Christians become actively involved in advancing the Kingdom of God or freeing captives from the dominion of Satan, they can expect heightened attacks by Satan's demonic forces, who will work hard to hinder their success. If you commit yourself to helping an SRA survivor obtain freedom from her spiritual bondages, you must therefore be prepared for this possibility. It need not evoke fear, however, as long as you understand the nature of the enemy, the battle, and the spiritual armor that can effectively foil his attacks.

As the reigning prince of the kingdom of darkness, Satan is a real being with supernatural power and intelligence, originally one of the highest created beings among the angelic hosts (Ezek. 28: 12-15). Having lost his personal challenge of God's supremacy in heaven (Isa. 14:12-15), his sights now seem to be set on gaining supremacy on earth. He and his grand following of demons are therefore pitted against God and His holy angels in a massive spiritual battle over the souls of mankind (Rev. 12:7-9). Both desire their loyal devotion but for very different reasons. While God desires an intimate love relationship with man, Satan desires only to use man to spite God and achieve his own grandiose scheme of world domination (1 John 5:29; Rev. 19:19).

While Satan may believe that he initiated his plan himself, God is the Mastermind behind his very existence. The absolute supremacy of God demands that He created, situated, and equipped Satan to serve His own purpose, which I believe is integrally entwined with the fulfillment of His own divine nature and the outworking of His ultimate plan for mankind.

The very essence of God's being is love, and throughout Scripture He is portrayed as a jealous suitor seeking the love and devotion of the people He created (Ex. 20:2-5; Deut. 13:1-5; Mat. 22:35-36; James 4:4, etc.). I believe, therefore, that God, who "*is love*" (1 John 4:8, 16) created man not only to be the object of His love (John 3:16), but also to enter into a reciprocating love relationship with Himself (Mark 12:30). He therefore created man in His own image (Gen. 1:27) with the unique ability to give and receive love.

While making man the object of His love was a unilateral decision on God's part, having a reciprocal love relationship with man requires a decision on our part as well. Even in purely human relationships we recognize that true love must be a carefully weighed and completely voluntary commitment of devotion to another. It is also most meaningful when the object of devotion is chosen from a playing field of other potentially appealing options. For this reason God not only created man with a free will but also provided an alternative object of devotion for him—which is how I believe Satan fits into His plan.

Because the choice God desired man to have would only be legitimate if the alternative was also a powerfully alluring, supernatural being, He created Satan as "the model of perfection, full of wisdom and perfect in beauty," abiding on the very "mount of God" (Ezek. 28:12-15). In this highly elevated position Satan felt so powerful and so privileged that he arrogantly aspired *to be like God*. He therefore rebelled against serving God and instead set his course on challenging His supremacy— and thus began his grand competition with God!

His immediate defeat in heaven focused Satan's sights on the earthly realm (Isaiah 14:12-15), which I believe was exactly God's plan. Even in the demotion that Satan suffered, however, God allowed him to have substantial resources and authority so that he would remain a viable competitor for the devotion of mankind. Satan therefore has a vast following of "evil spirits" or "demons" under his command as well as a limited, temporary authority over both the spiritual dimension known in Scripture as the "kingdom of the air" and the world system of government (Eph. 2:1-2; 1 John 5:19; Psalm 2:1-2; Rev. 11:15).

Through his victory in the Garden of Eden, Satan gained additional advantages in his competitive quest for the devotion of mankind. Because Adam and Eve, our ancient ancestors, chose to believe Satan rather than to obey God, all of mankind fell under the dominion of Satan (Rom. 6:16; 1 Cor. 15:20). Through this historic event Satan also gained direct access to man's deep, inner drives through the flesh (Rom. 8:7; Gal. 5:16-21). In other words, at this point man's sin nature was activated—which illustrates another dynamic which God built into man in His effort to make His competition with Satan fair. He made man not only with the ability to love, but with the ability to sin as well.

With every succeeding generation of mankind being born, by default, into the kingdom of darkness and having an inherent sin nature manifesting itself through the flesh, the deck seemed to become quickly stacked in Satan's favor. We must not be fooled into thinking that God lost His sovereignty over the entire situation, however. The Book of Job wondrously pulls back the curtain of heaven and allows us to see how God delights in having man still choose devotion to Himself even after He has conceded tremendous advantages to Satan.

Once man makes his decision to enter the mutual love relationship which God offers and is redeemed by the shed blood of Jesus (John 1:12; Eph. 1:7), God immediately turns the tables on Satan in our individual lives, however, and stacks the deck against him. God not only frees us from Satan's dominion (Col. 1:14), but also equips us for victory over Satan in all his avenues of operation.

Immediately upon salvation we receive the gift of the indwelling Holy Spirit (Rom. 8:9; 1 Cor. 6:19). Through this awesome transaction God shares with us His own divine nature, giving us the capacity to overcome both the sinful drives of the flesh and the illusive attraction of our corrupt world (Gal. 5:16; 2 Pet. 1:3-4).

God also graciously shares with us the mind of Christ through which He imparts His own divine wisdom. This wisdom is able to confound the wisdom of the world and tear down the strongholds which the enemy establishes in the hearts and minds of unbelievers (and possibly believers) to blind them to the truths of God (1 Cor. 1:18-2:16; 2 Cor. 4:3-4; 10:3-5; Eph. 1:17-18; James 3:13-17).

God even shares with us the position of spiritual authority over all the powers of darkness that He has granted to the risen Lord Jesus Christ in the heavenly realm (Eph. 1:19-23; 2:6). Once we recognize an attack, we can therefore use the authority of the name of Jesus Christ to command the obedience of any demonic forces that Satan deploys to fulfill specific assignments in our lives or environment (Luke 10:17; Acts 16:18).

Because Satan knows he has no chance against such a powerful *offensive* blow, he works very craftily to weaken our spiritual defenses and then camouflage his arrows so they sneak in unnoticed. For this reason God clearly instructs us how to put on a spiritual suit of armor which will effectively protect us from demonic attacks, however subtle or disguised they may be (Eph. 6:10-17).

If we are to keep Satan's arrows from piercing our souls and debilitating our effectiveness in the spiritual battle, we must understand the nature of each piece of the spiritual armor and how to keep all of them effectively in place. This armor is not an automatic inheritance which we receive at the time of salvation, or God would not instruct us to "put it on." It is also not something we can choose to put on "once and for all" subsequent to salvation.

Rather, the spiritual armor represents specific character qualities which we must develop and consistently apply in our daily lives. The extent to which we do determines the effectiveness of our defense against Satan. When we fail, we give Satan a potential opportunity to blindside us.

The Belt of Truth

Scripture describes Satan as a **liar** (John 8:44) and a **deceiver** (Rev. 12:9), yet one who disguises himself as an "angel of light" (2 Cor. 11:14). He is extremely adept at transforming lies to appear as truth, garbing them with tantalizing allurement, and expertly camouflaging their diabolical source as he did so well in the Garden of Eden (Gen. 3:1-5). He loves to implant niggling doubts, subtle half-truths, false condemnations, unfounded fears, and deceptive thoughts in our minds to diminish our spiritual strength. His tactics are so smooth that without keen sensitivity in our spirits we might easily attribute the origin of these inner messages to ourselves (Mat. 16:22-23; 2 Cor. 10:5; James 3:14-16).

If you enter a supportive relationship with an SRA survivor, Satan will undoubtedly seek an opportunity to direct his arrows of deception at both of you. Because the survivor's system of alter-identities experiences life in both the external world and a vast "inner world" of mental imagery, which is also accessible by Satan, she is vulnerable to his distortions of truth in both realms.

Internally, Satan can create or alter imagery to distract or divert alters from the truth needed for healing. Through false imagery or disguised demons he can deceive alters into believing they are obeying God when they are really following the will and directives of demons. Even apart from internal imagery, demons can emulate the "voice" of God and convey false messages as if from the true God. Survivors must therefore learn to test the source of internal messages and imagery by asking God to reveal its true nature.

In the survivor's external life Satan can implant erroneous thoughts, beliefs, and fears designed to cripple her healing. These may rob her of the supernatural peace, joy, and confidence which are hers as a child of God through the Holy Spirit (Gal. 5:22-23), leaving her instead with depression, fear, anxiety, and doubt of God's acceptance, love, and care. Other lies may undermine her sense of self-worth, position before God, or worthiness of His forgiveness. They may instill an exaggerated sense of guilt, shame, or defilement. Some may drive her to hopelessness, despair, or even suicide.

The survivor may be so blinded by Satan that she fails to recognize the demonic source of these thoughts and emotions. Therefore, if you, as a supporter, can keep this possibility in mind, you can be extremely helpful to her by gently suggesting the possibility of their Satanic origin and joining her in appropriate spiritual warfare. An immediate change in her mental or emotional state will indicate that your perception was right.

You must also be aware that Satan may attempt to attack *your* mind with his insidious lies as well. He may, for instance, try to excite fears and false suspicions of either the survivor or the cult to make you withdraw from your role as a supporter. Another tactic he might use is to instigate doubts of your adequacy to be of service to the survivor. If he cannot pull you completely away, he may try, through other implanted lies, to diminish your effectiveness in helping her.

Because Satan's tactics are so strongly based on deception, God tells us to gird ourselves with the **Belt of Truth**. Truth is one of the strongest weapons against Satan in the spiritual realm. He cannot stand against truth, especially the truths of God's Word. Through quoted Scripture alone Jesus totally defeated Satan when tempted by him in the wilderness (Mat. 4:1-11).

We can do the same, but only as we build a personal arsenal of truth in our own minds. For this reason God instructs us to meditate on His Word daily so we can hide its truths in our hearts (Josh. 1:8; Ps. 1:2; Ps. 119:11). The more we know of God's truth, the better equipped we will be in recognizing and refuting Satan's deceptions.

In order to gain the full protection of the **Belt of Truth**, we must not only *know* truth, however. We must also *practice* it (James 1:21-25). We must allow it to so transform our minds (Rom. 12:2) and direct the course of our daily lives (Ps. 119:105) that it becomes a distinguishing mark of our character. To whatever extent we fail in this regard, our spiritual defense is weakened, providing a potential foothold for the enemy.

Perhaps the most vulnerable and critical aspect of our lives to be governed by truth is our speech. James aptly describes the key role that speech plays in reflecting moral character and directing the course of one's life (James 3:2-6). For this reason it is one of Satan's prime targets. What destruction he can reap in and through our lives if we do not carefully guard our speech and keep it consistently in line with truth!

Jesus makes His standard for our speech very clear in Matthew 5:37: "Simply let your 'Yes' be 'Yes,' and 'No,' 'No'; anything beyond this *comes from the evil one.*" How much more blatantly could He declare that even the slightest deviation from truth in our speech comes from Satan, who is truly the "father of lies" (John 8:44)? When we yield to Satan's temptation to bend the truth, we essentially trade our **Belt of Truth** for one of Satan's key artillery pieces—deception (James 3:6).

Satan, of course, is delighted to lend us one of his weapons, especially in exchange for part of our defensive armor. However, he rarely lends out a piece of his artillery without one of his "soldiers" (demons) hovering nearby to coach us in its use. The more accustomed we become to using dishonesty, the more comfortable it feels and the deeper Satan digs his foothold in our soul.

With diabolical astuteness Satan gives us seemingly legitimate reasons to justify twisting the truth "just a little." Some may even seem godly in nature. Maybe we don't want to offend someone or "rock the boat." Perhaps we believe it will shelter or protect someone from pain or embarrassment—maybe even ourselves. We may start altering or exaggerating the truth to make a greater impact on people, seeing no harm in misrepresenting a situation as long as it doesn't hurt anyone.

These are all lies of the enemy! We must trust God that absolute truth is *always* the right thing in *every* situation. When we are obedient to Him in speaking truth, we can trust Him with the consequences.

Truth is most powerful when spoken in love (Eph. 4:15). If we use truth to shame, humiliate, or embarrass someone or deliver it with vengeful anger, we mix the godly power of truth with fleshly characteristics tainted by the enemy. This sends greatly conflicting messages and rarely produces positive results.

The Breastplate of Righteousness

Although sin no longer determines our eternal destiny once we have been redeemed by the blood of Christ, it has a major impact on our spiritual health and the integrity of our spiritual armor. One of Satan's greatest strategies is therefore to lead us to sin. He knows that sin will hinder our intimacy with God and access to His power through prayer (Ps. 24:3-5; 34:15-16; 66:18; 1 John 1:6-7).

Willfully engaging in sin (James 4:17) is so crippling to our strength in the spiritual battle that it is seemingly analogous to exposing our heart to the enemy. For this reason God instructs us to keep our life-sustaining chest area covered with the **Breastplate of Righteousness**. Since this is a righteousness that we are to "put on" (Eph. 6:14; NASB), I believe that it refers to the consistent practice of righteousness in our daily lives rather than the righteousness of Christ with which we are permanently covered when we place our faith in Him for salvation (Rom. 5:1).

While living a totally sinless life is an impossible goal, God has graciously provided every resource we need to maintain our spiritual protection of righteousness. We, however, must learn to utilize these resources effectively in order to keep our breastplate firmly in place.

Before salvation we are all in bondage to our sin nature. No amount of human effort can free us from it. However, as soon as we accept Jesus Christ as our personal Savior from sin, He instantly frees us from that bondage. We are cleansed by the blood of Jesus and given the gift of the Holy Spirit, who indwells us (1 Cor. 6:19; 2 Cor. 1:21-22; 5:5).

Our hearts now hear the beat of two drummers, one coming from the flesh, which continues to throb with the deceptive allurements of self-gratification, and the other from the Holy Spirit, who yearns to synchronize our spirits with His own divine nature. Our job is to learn to distinguish the two, resist the lustful pulsations of the flesh, and allow the Holy Spirit to be the true "drum major" of our lives. Only then can we successfully escape the corruption of our flesh as well as the temptations of the evil one and the world system he operates (Rom. 8:5-6; Gal. 5:16-17; Eph. 2:1-3; 2 Pet. 1:3-4).

While sin is sometimes blatantly obvious, at other times it can be very subtle and even camouflaged as a seeming righteousness. Satan is quite masterful in counterfeiting the righteousness of God in a person's life. The Pharisees in the Gospels, whom Jesus called "son[s] of hell" (Mat. 23:15), are a prime example of this false righteousness as they willfully aligned their behavior to a rabbinical code of conduct. The roots of their seemingly godly lifestyle were deeply entangled in their prideful flesh, however.

Christians today can fall into this same legalistic trap if they concentrate on merely following godly "rules" of conduct rather than allowing true righteousness to flow spontaneously from a heart submitted to the Holy Spirit. While subtle, this important difference can significantly affect one's spiritual strength against the enemy (Gal. 3:1-5).

In addition to the Holy Spirit, another vitally important resource for keeping our **Breastplate of Righteousness** consistently in place is the Word of God. Studying it on a daily basis enables God's standard of righteousness to penetrate deep within our hearts and minds, purifying our lives and enhancing our ability to recognize sin (Josh. 1:8, Ps. 1:2; 119:9, 11; John 15:3).

Because we can never fully escape the alluring deceptions of the world, the flesh, and the devil in this life, even the most dedicated of Christians will fail to maintain a consistently sinless life (Rom. 7:15-25). When sin inevitably creeps in, however, God has additional resources which are instantly activated on our behalf. Not only does the indwelling Holy Spirit sound an alarm alerting us to the error of our ways (John 16:8), but Jesus Christ Himself steps before the Father's throne as our Advocate declaring that His shed blood covers our sin. All we have to do is be sensitive to the inner conviction of the Holy Spirit and confess our sin to God. When we do, our fellowship with Him and our privileges before His throne are instantly restored, and our **Breastplate of Righteousness** is returned to its protective position against the assaults of the enemy (1 John 1:6—2:2).

The Boots of Peace

Sturdy, protective footwear enables a soldier to brace himself against an enemy attack or maneuver quickly over rough terrain without damage to his feet. In spiritual warfare our battlefield boots are found in the full appropriation of the **Gospel of Peace**.

On a very foundational level our faith in the Gospel message of Jesus Christ's sacrificial death on the Cross for our sins secures our peace with God (Rom. 5:1). Our sins are forgiven and no longer separate us from Him. We are released from God's wrath, freed from Satan's dominion, and rest in the peace and assurance of our eternal destiny with God Himself (Rom. 6:22). This is a *positional* peace acquired "once and for all" through faith at the time of our salvation.

God also offers us a deep internal peace, however, which can sustain us through the most difficult of circumstances. This *experiential* peace is the footwear which provides our stability before the enemy. While it is always available to us, we play a key role in the degree to which it characterizes our lives (Isa. 26:3; Col. 3:15).

When we learn how to appropriate it, God's peace is a powerful antidote to the emotions of anger, anxiety, and fear, which make us particularly vulnerable to losing our grip spiritually and allowing Satan to gain a foothold in our lives (Gen. 4:6-7; Eph. 4:26). Strong emotions such as these can potentially overpower our mind's commitment to godliness, opening the door for our flesh to direct our actions instead. If we are to remain strong in the spiritual battle, we must become adept at exchanging these natural reactions to life's problems for God's peace.

The first step is to become increasingly attuned to recognizing when our emotions have robbed us of peace. The quicker we catch ourselves and remedy the situation, the less time we will spend "bootless" on slippery terrain before our enemy.

Anger

Anger is a particularly volatile emotion which can erupt either as a natural response to a wrong suffered or as a fleshly reaction due to jealousy, envy, perfectionistic expectations, or selfish demands for our own way (Gal. 5:19-20). In either case anger puts us into an extremely vulnerable position spiritually with Satan "crouching at the door" and wooing us to succumb to his will (Gen. 4:5-7). God never condemns anger but strongly warns us not to allow our anger to lead us to commit sin or to become an ongoing bitterness in our lives (Eph. 4:26-27; James 1:20). Instead He urges us to try to live in peace with all men (Rom. 14:19; Heb. 12:14-15).

When someone has truly wronged us, the path to peace ultimately lies in forgiving that person (Mark 11:25; Eph. 4:32) by relinquishing all desires for vengeance to God (Gen. 18:25; Rom. 12:19; Col. 3:25). Through forgiveness God allows us to rid ourselves of the emotional burden of determining and executing the just fate of our offender by taking that responsibility on Himself. Forgiveness is His gift to us, enabling us to experience peace and emotional health in spite of being grievously wronged. (See p. 32

for a fuller description of the relationship between anger, hate, and forgiveness.)

When our anger stems from purely self-centered motives, we need a major change in attitude, which can often be achieved by asking ourselves how God or another objective person would look at the situation. When we recognize that our anger is rooted in pride, jealousy, or perfectionistic demands and surrender these ungodly character traits to God, His peace can once again replace our anger—and often defuse the external situation as well.

Anxiety

Anxiety is another natural emotional response that can easily disrupt our peace as we face the cares and chaos of this world. God does not promise to free us from such situations, but in the midst of the trials and troubles which will invariably come, He offers a supernatural oasis of peace for His children (John 16:33).

Securing this peace again requires studying God's Word (Ps. 119:65) so we can understand His character, His promises, and the nature of our relationship to Him. Because our loving Father abundantly provides for even the birds and flowers, He certainly will care for us who are of much greater value in His sight (Mat. 6:25-34; Phil. 4:19). He firmly declares that nothing can separate us from His love (Rom. 8:38-39). He even promises that if we walk in love and obedience to Him, He will make every situation that befalls us result in good (Gen. 50:20; Rom. 8:28). These are but a few of the unchangeable promises of God that form the bedrock foundation for the peace that He offers us (Heb. 6:17-19).

Living in peace also requires that we foster a dual awareness of both the physical and spiritual realms (2 Cor. 4:17-18; Col. 3:1-3). Anxieties increase if we focus only on the material realm and lose sight of all that transcends its finite limitations. The reality of God's constant presence with us and the powerful resources He makes available to us in the spiritual realm make a world of difference for the Christian when facing the challenges of life.

None of these benefits can effect peace on their own, however. Peace only comes when we are willing to place our faith fully in God and willfully relinquish our anxieties (1 Peter 5:7). If we can, by faith, rest secure in His sovereignty even in the direst of circumstances, He will give us His supernatural peace, which is so transforming that it defies understanding (Phil. 4:6-7).

Fear

Fear is another natural emotion that can quickly overtake us when our protective "antennae" sense any form of danger or we face a situation which can potentially threaten our life, security, or well-being. The peace-robbing peril may be real or imagined, anticipated or actually present. The less control we have in determining our fate in such situations, the stronger the potential for fear.

Again, the supernatural peace of God can serve as an antidote for our fears in a way unbelievers cannot possibly fathom (John 14:27). While it again requires a major act of faith on our part, it is marvelously effective whether our fears concern the physical or spiritual realm, natural calamities, frightening circumstances, or threatening human beings.

Fear of Satan and demons. What is unseen can be particularly frightening, especially if it is perceived as evil. Perhaps this is one reason why many people, including Christians, choose to live virtually oblivious to the spiritual realm—or at least the evil part of it. This is their way of coping with their fear of unseen, supernatural, evil beings existing around them. Some may try to convince themselves that demons exist only in the more heathen parts of the world or that if they ignore Satan and his forces, he too will ignore them. This is tragic because it leaves them in a much more vulnerable position with the enemy.

Fear of Satan and his demons is totally unnecessary for the believer. A soldier of Jesus Christ can stand firm in his spiritual **Boots of Peace** if he clearly understands his relationship to both the kingdom of darkness and the kingdom of God.

The relationship of Satan to those under his dominion is best described as a master over his *slaves*, which can rightfully evoke fear. However, when God delivers us from Satan's kingdom into His own through our faith in the blood of the Lord Jesus Christ (Col. 1:13-14), we become not his *slaves*, but His *children* (John 1:12; 1 John 3:1). He gives us a "spirit of adoption" by which we can cry out to Him as our loving, protecting Father. Paul urges us, as believers, to grasp the full reality of our glorious position as *children* of God and *joint heirs* with Jesus Christ and not transpose any of the fears of our previous relationship with Satan onto our new relationship with God (Rom. 8:15-17).

Because Satan moves from being our master to being our enemy when we change our allegiance to God, he can still be an object of fear—but only to an ignorant believer. When we clothe ourselves in the spiritual armor and use the authority which God has granted us in the spiritual realm, we can boldly command the obedience of Satan's forces in the powerful name of the Lord Jesus Christ (Luke 10:17; Acts 16:18; James 4:7). We need never cower before them. We have the means to be victorious over them one hundred percent of the time—*if* we keep ourselves spiritually vigilant to recognize their attacks (I Pet. 5:8).

Fear of death. One of the most powerful fears Satan captivates his subjects with is the fear of death. According to 1 John 4:18, "fear has to do with punishment." At some level of our being we all know that God exists, that He is holy, and that He upholds a standard of righteousness for mankind (Rom. 1:18-20; Lev. 19:2). If we fall short of that standard, we know that we deserve punishment. The punishment for sin established in the Garden of Eden and repeated over and over through Scripture is death (Gen. 2:16; 3:19, 22; Ezek. 18:4; Rom. 6:23, etc.). Therefore those who choose to remain under Satan's dominion live in bondage to the fear of death and the retribution for sin that lies beyond it (Heb. 2:14-15).

This is totally unnecessary for the child of God however. When Jesus died on the Cross, He took upon Himself the punishment for our sins. He suffered death in our place (1 Pet. 3:18). Through faith in His substitutionary death, we are therefore freed from the death penalty for our sins (John 3:16; 5:24; Rom. 8:1-2). While we will still die physically, we no longer have to *fear* death (Heb. 2:15). Its "sting" is removed (1 Cor. 15:55). Death no longer leads to eternal punishment but rather to a glorious inheritance reserved in heaven for us (1 Pet. 1:4)!

Fear of God's punishment. Although we need never fear the punishment of *death* for our sins, Scripture teaches that all believers will "appear before the judgment seat of Christ" to receive the just recompense for our deeds here on earth. At that time we will be rewarded or "suffer loss" according to how we lived our lives. Even the apostle Paul lived in sober anticipation of this day of judgment when each man's work will be made evident and tested by fire (Rom. 14:10-12; 1 Cor. 3:10-15; 2 Cor: 5:10-11).

Again, however, God amply supplies what we need to deliver us from the fear of future judgment at His hand. First John 4:16-18 explains that "perfect love" eliminates this fear. While only God exhibits such love on His own (1 John 4:8), He willingly shares *His own divine nature* with us through the union of His Spirit with ours at salvation (1 Cor. 6:17; Gal. 5:22; 2 Peter 1:4). To the extent that we allow it, God's perfect love can permeate and characterize *our* lives as well. When His love directs our thoughts, words, and actions, fear of His judgment is completely eliminated (1 John 4:12, 17).

If, on the other hand, we quench the manifestation of the Holy Spirit's love in and through our lives (1 Thes. 5:19) and choose instead to live according to the self-centered desires of the flesh, we cannot experience God's peace in our lives. The prospect of standing face to face with our Redeemer and accounting for our deeds rightfully creates both guilt and fear.

Fear of physical calamities. God's supernatural peace can supplant our fears in relationship to the natural realm as well as the spiritual realm. Our ability to secure that deep, inner serenity in all circumstances depends, however, on our grasping the truths of Scripture concerning the nature of God and His promises (Ps. 119:165). Only by holding tightly to these can we, by faith, exchange our *natural* fears for His *supernatural* peace.

When we fully appropriate God's peace, we can say with the psalmist, "God is our refuge and strength, an ever-present help in trouble. Therefore, we will not fear, though the earth give way and the mountains fall into the heart of the sea, though its waters roar and foam and the mountains quake with their surging" (Ps. 46:1-3). Even terrifying physical calamities, such as earthquakes, hurricanes, tornadoes, and floods, occur within the scope of God's sovereignty and control. He is fully able to deliver us from all harm in the midst of these disasters if He chooses to do so (Mark 4:36-41; Ps. 91).

Our peace does not depend on God's protection, however. Our peace is based on the assurance that nothing can separate us from Him and His love—not even death (Rom. 8:38-39)! No matter how devastating a catastrophe befalls us, we know that God will either protect us, sustain us by His love and all-sufficient grace (Heb. 4:16), or usher us victoriously into His presence (Ps. 23:4)! *"Whether we live or die, we are the Lord's"* (Rom. 14:8)!

Fear of difficult circumstances. These unchangeable truths can carry us peacefully through frightening circumstances precipitated by human actions as well. Nothing that happens to us is ever out of God's sight or the scope of His sovereignty. He is aware of every detail of our lives and vitally concerned about each one (Ps. 31:14-15; 139:1-18; Mat. 10:29-31). *Resting by faith in the absolute security of our personal relationship to God as a loving Father is the secret which enables us to have peace in a world filled with tribulation* (Isa. 26:3; John 14:27; 16:33; Rom. 8:15).

While no circumstance is ever too difficult for God to overcome on our behalf (Jer. 32:17), He sometimes chooses to use frightening or difficult situations to strengthen our faith in Him and develop our character (James 1:2-4; Rom. 5:3-4). Our faith can only grow when we confront situations that surpass what we can handle with our human capabilities alone. Only when we are thrust totally on God can He prove His faithfulness to us, either by miraculously delivering us (2 Cor. 1:8-10) or by supernaturally equipping us to handle the trying situation (2 Cor. 3:5; 4:7; 12:9-10).

God promises not only that He will never abandon us (Heb. 13:5-6), but also that He will work in every situation for the good of those who love Him and walk obediently in His will (Rom. 8:28). When we truly grasp the reality of these magnificent promises, we can choose to walk in peace through whatever trials He allows in our lives.

Fear of threatening people. Encountering people who seemingly have the power to hurt, humiliate, or take advantage of us in some way is another situation which naturally evokes fear. Again, however, God gives us the resources to overcome such fear and replace it with His supernatural peace. Often this begins by recognizing that we may be up against more than human dynamics in these situations.

Although we know that God performs much of the work of His kingdom through the Holy Spirit indwelling and empowering His children, we often fail to recognize that Satan can work in a similar way through those in *his* kingdom. Therefore, what we may perceive as a human conflict may actually be propelled or augmented by demonic forces. If we learn to approach fearsome people in this manner, our confidence can often be boosted because we know that He that is in us is greater than any of Satan's forces (1 John 4:4). We also know that we can at least temporarily halt demonic agendas and protect ourselves through spiritual warfare. While verbally rebuking demons we suspect may be working through the other person may not be wise, we can do so under our breath or silently ask God to do so.

Of course, we can't blame all human conflicts on the direct involvement of demons, but God has additional resources available to us in such situations as well. He reminded Timothy, when he was apparently fearful of persecution by those who were opposed to the Gospel message, that He has not given us a "spirit of timidity, but a spirit of **power**, of **love** and of **discipline**" (2 Tim. 1:7). Each of these spiritual endowments is somehow designed to counterbalance fear when dealing with hostile people.

Most Christians greatly underestimate the **power** that God makes available to those who believe. Ephesians 1:19-21 says this power is the same power that raised Jesus Christ from the dead and placed Him in a position of authority at the Father's right hand far above all created beings. Ephesians 3:20 says that God "is able to do immeasurably more than all we ask or imagine, according to his power that is at work within us" (Eph. 3:20).

This unfathomable outpouring of God's power into our lives is probably limited only by the degree of our ignorance, arrogance, lack of faith, or failure to request it. When we try to handle things with our own strength and abilities, God usually lets us do that. However, when we are willing to acknowledge our own inadequacies and surrender to the total sufficiency of God's enablement (2 Cor. 3:5), we open the door for His power to operate in us. In God's family when we are weak, then we are strong. This principle enabled Paul to stand firmly in his **Boots** of Peace even when evil men insulted and persecuted him. He was confident that these were opportunities to see the power of God work marvelously on his behalf (2 Cor. 12:9-10). By faith we can stand in that same confidence.

Yielding ourselves fully to God enables not only His power, but also His **love,** to flow through our lives (Rom. 5:5; 1 John 4:12). As His love grips and motivates our hearts, our evangelistic zeal (2 Cor. 5:14-15) will supersede our fear of persecution, suffering, and humiliation as we boldly live and work for the cause of Christ (2 Tim. 1:7-8; Phil. 3:7-8).

When God's love flows through us, it is also apt to transform our "people skills" so that we are not only less likely to antagonize fearsome people, but we are also able to disarm them with a kind and gentle spirit (1 Cor. 13:4-7; Luke 6:27-28). According to Scripture love can extinguish wrath, overcome evil, and bring conviction to our enemies (Prov. 15:1; Rom. 12:20).

The indwelling Holy Spirit also enhances our ability to **discipline** ourselves to follow a consistent, committed lifestyle patterned after Christ Himself regardless of the circumstances or people confronting us (Gal. 5:22-23; Titus 2:11-12). Without this, we are apt to respond to frightening people through our flesh, further enflaming the confrontation. When our own resolve for godliness is coupled with the enabling power of the Holy Spirit, however, we can stand boldly, confidently, and peacefully before threatening people, which can amazingly disarm them. Scripture clearly states that when our trust is in God, we need not fear what man can do to us (Ps. 27:1; 56:4; Heb. 13:5-6).

Through the abundant resources that God makes available to us, we can experience His supernatural peace in any situation. Our success in doing so depends on our consistent awareness of His loving and powerful presence with us and the degree of faith we are willing to exercise in relinquishing our fears in exchange for God's peace. We are never out of His sight, love, and sovereignty—no matter what situation we face, whether "trouble or hardship or persecution or famine or nakedness or danger or sword. . . . In all these things we are more than conquerors through Him who loved us" (Rom. 8:35-39; cf. 139:1-18; 31:51a). The "shadow of the Almighty" is always our place of refuge, and within it we find incredible security and peace (Ps. 91:1).

The Shield of Faith

Faith is not only the means through which we enter the Kingdom of God; it is the basis of the entire Christian life (Rom. 1:17; Gal. 2:20; 2 Cor. 5:7). As such, it is vitally important in our defense against the enemy. The more areas in which we exercise it, the more protection it offers us in the spiritual realm. In the armor it is aptly represented as the moveable shield, able to cover most any part of the body.

As the shield, faith supports and reinforces the effectiveness of the other pieces of the armor. For instance, we receive our **salvation** and are delivered from the kingdom of darkness by faith (Eph. 2:8; Col. 1:13-14). With our sins forgiven, we stand by faith in the surety of our possession of Christ's **righteousness** whenever Satan hurls false accusations, guilt, and thoughts of unworthiness at us (Phil. 3:9).

By faith we appropriate the fullness of the Holy Spirit in our lives and allow Him to direct us in **righteousness** rather than falling victim to the evil desires of our flesh (Gal. 3:2-5, 14; 5:16, 25). By faith we claim the promises of Scripture and the magnitude of our inheritance in the *spiritual* realm, causing the sinful allurements of our *materialistic* world to fade in importance (1 Cor. 4:18; 1 John 5:4). This strengthens our ability to continue walking by faith in **righteousness** even in the midst of trials (James 1:2-4; Rom. 5:3-5) when we see no evidence of God's presence (2 Cor. 4:17; 5:7; Heb. 11:1; 1 Pet. 1:8).

By faith we accept the **truths** of Scripture and align our lives with them (Ps. 119:105). Faith also emboldens us to proclaim those **truths** to Satan, instantly melting him in his tracks (Mat. 4:1-11). By faith we resist Satan's attempts to lure us into speaking any form of falsehood (Mat. 5:37), believing that God always honors **truth** (Ps. 24:3-5).

Only by faith can we truly appropriate the **peace** of God and allow it to characterize our lives and relationships (Col. 3:15). Relinquishing our naturally occurring anger, anxiety, and fear and exchanging them for God's supernatural **peace** takes a tremendous act of faith, but it prevents these emotions from potentially becoming footholds for Satan (Eph. 4:26-27). If we can hold tightly, by faith, to the security of our relationship to God as a loving Father (Rom. 8:35-39), no situation in the natural or spiritual realm can rob us of God's **peace** (John 14:27; 16:33), not even the threat of death, which is one of Satan's most powerful tactics (Heb. 2:14-15; Rev. 2:10). Allowing God's love and power to be perfected in us is also an act of faith, which further diminishes fear and anxiety and enhances **peace** in our lives (2 Cor. 12:9; 1 John 4:17).

By faith we rely on God supplying the **Sword of the Spirit**, which is the internally spoken **Word of God**, whenever we need it to confront evil (Acts 13:8-12; Eph. 6:17). By faith we do not shrink from articulating this **Word of God** whenever it is given, even under persecution (Luke 21:12-15; 1 Pet. 3:15).

Faith is the vital factor which unleashes in our lives the same power that raised Jesus Christ from the dead and placed Him in the position of supreme authority over all the powers of darkness (Eph. 1:19-23). Because God graciously allows us, as His children, to share this position with Christ, we can by faith use the authority of the name of Jesus to overcome Satan's forces too (Eph. 2:6). Satan may roar like a lion, seeking to intimidate and take advantage of us, but as long as we remain spiritually alert and boldly raise our **Shield of Faith** to resist him, he will flee from us (Eph. 6:16; 1 Peter 5:8-9; James 4:7).

Because our faith is so important in the spiritual battle, God deliberately works to build and strengthen it while Satan seeks to destroy it (1 Thes. 3:2-10; 2 Cor. 1:8-10; James 1:3-4; 1 Peter 1:6-9). The Book of Job is an excellent example of how God and Satan are pitted against each other in challenging and testing the strength of man's faith.

When faith is genuine, it transforms our lives and is demonstrated by our actions (James 2:14-26). Living a life of faith doesn't necessarily mean that we perform great miracles, but rather that we obey God's commandments and do His will, following the example of Jesus' life on earth (Mat. 7:15-23; 1 John 2:3-6). True faith spawns a deep love for God and people, which is evident to those around us (John 13:35; 1 John 4:20; James 2:15-16; Mat. 25:34-46).

Faith also plays a key role in prayer. Because prayer is the powerful lifeline which allows us to have direct access to God and His awesome resources, Satan probably rejoices when our faith in prayer diminishes. Therefore, instead of allowing our faith to shrink when God seemingly fails to answer our prayers, we must try to understand *why*.

The reason most likely lies with the inappropriateness of our requests or the manner in which we brought them to God rather than in any unfaithfulness on God's part.

John 14:13 reveals two key principles which are very instructive concerning effective prayer. First Jesus gives us the privilege of using the authority of His name in our prayers, and then He promises to answer all requests which bring glory to the Father.

The privilege of praying "in Jesus' name" is something we must never take lightly. It means much more than tacking His name ritualistically onto the end of our prayers. God's solemn command not to misuse His name (Ex. 20:7) still bears relevance to our lives today and must certainly apply to our prayers.

In Biblical times one's name represented his complete identity or overall character, somewhat similar to the authority of our signature today. Therefore to live in blatant disregard of the character of Christ and yet pray "in His name" dreadfully misuses it. We can only truly pray "in His name" when our hearts are in line with His. The model prayer which Jesus taught His disciples begins with an expression of agreement with the will of God (Mat. 6:10).

The more we can personally identify with the character, motivations, priorities, and desires of Jesus, the more we fulfill the other requirements for effective prayer given throughout Scripture as well. For instance, we cannot align our hearts with Christ without confessing all known sin (James 5:16; 1 John 3:21-23) and allowing God's Word to be a living and active reality in our daily lives (John 15:7). Tuning our hearts to the heart of Christ will also bring our requests in line with His will (1 John 5:14-15) and strengthen our faith that God will truly answer them (James 1:6-8; Heb. 10:22; 11:6).

Equally as important as how we pray is the nature of the requests we bring to God. In John 14:13 Jesus promised to answer those requests that bring glory to God. The context in which this promise is given, along with other Scriptures on the subject, seem to indicate that God is particularly glorified by our gaining spiritual maturity and continuing Jesus' ministry on earth (John 14:12-14; 15:8; Phil. 1:9-11; 2 Thes. 1:11-13). Therefore we can confidently expect God to answer sincere requests to facilitate the accomplishment of these goals in and through our lives.

In addition to the effect that our requests will have on God, another criterion that God establishes concerns the effect they will have on us or the one for whom we are praying. Because God created us to have a reciprocal love relationship with Himself and is competing with Satan for our devotion, He will never answer prayers that arise from our fleshly nature and that will draw us closer to the world than to Himself (James 4:3-5).

Within those broad parameters lie many possibilities. While we are most assured of God answering prayers which relate to the work of the Kingdom and bring glory to Him, Scripture also gives repeated instructions or examples of believers praying for healing (James 5:14-16), relief from troubling circumstances (Phil. 4:6-7; Heb. 4:15-16; James 5:13), protection (Neh. 4:6-9; Ps. 6:6-10; Ezra 8:21-23; John 17:11-15), adversarial relationships (Mat. 5:44; Luke 6:28; 18:1-7), their country (Ps. 122:6; Jer. 29:7; 1 Tim. 2:1-2), the gift of children (1 Sam. 1:1-20), and the right marriage partner (Gen. 24). These inspired examples indicate the appropriateness of seeking God's intervention in these areas as well.

When we bring our requests to God, we must remember, however, that God's perspective is infinitely broader than ours and His plans wiser (Isa. 55:8-9). Therefore when God does not answer a seemingly legitimate request for which we earnestly plead, we must believe that He is still acting true to His character and with our best welfare in mind. This too requires faith.

We must also remember that although God is always *able* to intervene on our behalf and override the natural laws and spiritual principles by which He designed His creation to operate, He is never *obligated* to do so, nor do we ever *deserve* such a response. When He grants our requests, He does so as an extension of His grace. However, in His love and compassion for us, He *invites us* to come boldly before His throne and receive His *grace* and *mercy* in our time of need (Heb. 4:14-16).

As any loving father, God is eager to give good gifts to His children, even beyond what we ask—sometimes even beyond our greatest imaginations (Matt. 7:9-11; Eph. 3:20; James 1:17; Ps. 84:11). When our hearts genuinely find their delight in Him, Scripture says that He will graciously and lovingly fulfill the desires of our hearts (Ps. 37:4). What a Father! Praise His holy name!

The Helmet of Salvation

A soldier entering a military battle without a helmet would be regarded as insane. The head is one of the most critical areas to protect as it is the control center of the entire body. Entering the spiritual battle without the **Helmet of Salvation** is just as dangerous. Scripture vividly recounts that when the unsaved sons of Sceva attempted to cast out a demon in the name of Jesus, they were overpowered and beaten so badly that they "ran out of the house naked and bleeding" (Acts 19:13-16).

Apart from our personal **salvation** through the blood of Jesus Christ, we have no grounds at all for defeating Satan. While Jesus died for the sins of the whole world, we must individually accept His death on the Cross of Calvary as the full payment for *our* sins (John 1:12; 3:16-18). This is the crucial act that translates us out of Satan's dominion into the Kingdom of God (Col. 1:13-14), where we are seated with Christ in the heavenly realm far above all the forces of darkness (Eph. 1:19-21; 2:4). In this position we are granted the privilege of using the power and authority of Jesus' name to defeat the forces of the evil one whenever we recognize their presence (Luke 10:17; Acts 16:18; Rev. 12:11).

Because of the foundational role that **salvation** plays in our ability to command the obedience of Satan and his forces in the name of Jesus, we might expect the **Helmet of Salvation** to be listed first among the pieces of the armor. Instead it is almost the last piece mentioned. Rather than reflecting a lack of importance, however, its placement near the end of the list may be more indicative of its low maintenance requirement. Putting on the **Helmet of Salvation** does not require daily vigilance or effort on our part. Instead, this part of the armor is given to us purely as a gift from God (according to the meaning of the Greek word translated "take" in this verse). How gracious of God to make the vital protection of our head depend not on our efforts but on His free and everlasting gift to us (Rom. 6:23)!

The Sword of the Spirit

The **Sword of the Spirit** is the only offensive weapon included in the spiritual armor. Like the **Helmet of Salvation**, it too is given to us as a gift from God. He will faithfully provide it in our moment of need. Our responsibility is to learn to rely on its availability and not grasp for any fleshly substitute when confronting the enemy.

While the **Sword of the Spirit** is quickly identified as the Word of God, the Greek word used refers specifically to the *spoken* Word of God. This means that at certain critical times God promises to give us the words that will effectively counteract the assault of the enemy. He intends that the **Sword of the Spirit** not only to strike with supernatural power, but also to free us from anxiety over choosing our own words at those adrenalin pumping times (Mat. 10:16-20; Luke 21:12-15). The **Sword of the Spirit** is thus another resource graciously given by God to enable us to maintain our **Boots of Peace** as well.

Whether we stand before rulers for the sake of the Gospel or confront demonized individuals (Acts 13:6-12), our responsibility is to be sensitive to the inner voice of the Holy Spirit and boldly deliver the words He gives us. When we do, we can be assured that those divinely chosen words will be such that "none of [our] adversaries will be able to resist or contradict" (Luke 21:15).

Conclusion

Keeping ourselves safe in the spiritual battle requires a unique partnership with God. While He freely gives us the **Helmet of Salvation** and the **Sword of the Spirit,** we are responsible for keeping the other pieces of the spiritual armor in sound working condition, drawing upon the totally sufficient resources which God supplies. This entails being knowledgeable of Scripture, aware of the spiritual realm, attuned to the Holy Spirit, committed to godliness, and willing to exercise faith in God's promises. When our lives are consistently characterized by truth, righteousness, peace, and faith, the arrows Satan aims at us will be instantly deflected, finding no resting place.

Appendix A

Definition of Terms

ABREACTION—The recall of a traumatic memory in such vivid sensory and affective form that it seems like a re-experiencing of the event.

ACCESS—Direct or indirect contact of a programmed cult member through physical or electronic means, predetermined signals, programmed triggers, or spiritual beings.

AFFECT—A psychological term referring to emotions.

ALTER—An abbreviated form of "alternate personality" or "alternate identity"; a part of the person that is separated by dissociation from the Core.

ALTER-IDENTITY—A part of the person that is separated by dissociation from the Core; may, or may not, have a completely developed personality of its own; often used interchangeably with "alter-personality."

ALTER-PERSONALITY—A part of the person that is separated by dissociation from the Core and has a relatively enduring pattern of perceiving, thinking about, and relating to self, others, and the environment.

ALTERED STATE OF CONSCIOUSNESS—Any shift of the focus of one's attention away from a clear connectedness to the immediate external environment.

AMNESIA—The inability to recall significant events or other important information which is too extreme to be explained by ordinary forgetfulness; the absence of memory, usually experienced in DID to some extent between certain identities.

BODY MEMORY—The re-experiencing of the pain or physical sensations of a past traumatic event or the re-appearance of physical bruises, marks, or wounds on the body from such an event.

BLACK-OUT—A loss of consciousness which is experienced by a particular identity while another identity is in executive control of the body.

CO-CONSCIOUSNESS—The phenomenon of more than one identity sharing an awareness of external life at the same time, having varying degrees of influence on the control of the body; usually refers to the Host maintaining an awareness of events which transpire when other identities take executive control of the body.

CONDITIONING—The process by which a consistent behavioral pattern is established in response to a given stimulus.

CORE—The personality which is most directly related to the whole person conceived in the womb; carries the strongest sense of "self."

CORE SPLIT—A first generation alter-personality dissociatively separated directly from the Core.

CULT—An organized group of people devoted to beliefs and goals which are not held by the majority of society; often religious in nature. In this book, used to refer to an organized, covert perpetrator group

CULTIST—Any perpetrator who is part of an organized group of people devoted to a specific covert agenda not shared by the general population.

DARKNESS—Satan's realm, usually associated with evil and deception.

DELIVERANCE—The process of freeing a person or alter-identity from demonization.

DEMON—An evil spirit associated with Satan and his agenda.

DEMONIZATION—Varying degrees of demonic control or influence over a person or alter.

DISSOCIATE—To separate all or part of one's consciousness from connection to the external environment; in DID the act of splitting one's mind into separate identities.

DISSOCIATION—A disruption or separation in the usually integrated functions of consciousness, memory, identity, or perception of the environment.[5] This phenomenon lies on a continuum ranging from normal day dreaming and "highway hypnosis" on one end to the extremely pathological formation of alternate-identities (DID) at the other end.

DISSOCIATIVE—Having the ability to dissociate or being characterized by dissociation.

DISSOCIATIVE IDENTITY DISORDER (DID)—The new official term for what was formerly known as Multiple Personality Disorder; "the presence of two or more distinct identities or personality states (each with its own relatively enduring pattern of perceiving, relating to, and thinking about the environment and self)" within a single person, two of which "recurrently take control of the individual's behavior."[6]

EXECUTIVE CONTROL—The ability to determine the actions of the body.

FOOTHOLD—The legal ground that gives a demon the right to influence a person or alter-identity. This could be an oath, vow, pledge, ritual, sacrifice, generational inheritance, or specific sin.

FRAGMENT—An alter-identity with a limited life-history and function who does not have a fully developed personality.

FUSION—The merging of two alter-identities so that they become one. Technically this reversal of the dissociation process is differentiated from "integration" in that neither of the merging identities is the Core.

GENEALOGICAL MAP—A flow-chart showing the derivation of the alter-identities as they split off from the Core or other alters.

GENERATIONAL SATANISM—Satanism which is propagated through succeeding generations.

HOST—The presenter personality who is most often in executive control of the body. This can change over the course of the individual's life.

IDENTITY—A person's distinct sense of self; used in DID to refer to each divided part of the soul created by dissociation; is sometimes used interchangeably with "personality."

INNER SELF HELPER (ISH)—An alter-identity who is devoted to the good of the person and works to maintain internal stability and well-being; may provide helpful information to guide the therapist; rarely participates in external life.

INNER WORLD (or INTERNAL LANDSCAPE)—A seemingly internal realm of mental imagery, often representing the system map, where some identities may interact with each other when they are not participating in external life. This realm can apparently intersect with spiritual dimensions allowing demonic interaction with the alters.

INTEGRATION—The process of joining alter-identities back into the Core personality.

LAYER—A group of alters who are loosely related and aware of each other, who may have participated in life together at one time. Multiple layers of alters usually exist in a system beneath the current group of presenters. In survivors of Satanic Ritual Abuse these are often strategically positioned to reinforce the programming and provide additional defenses against therapeutic intrusions.

LOSS OF TIME—The phenomenon of time passing for which the Host or a particular alter-identity is amnestic.

MULTIPLE—A person with multiple identities; someone diagnosed with Dissociative Identity Disorder.

MULTIPLE PERSONALITY DISORDER (MPD)—The former title for the psychological diagnosis now known as "Dissociative Identity Disorder."

ORIGINAL PERSON—The person created at conception from which the first alter-identities were split; often used synonymously with Core.

OCCULT—Hidden or secret practices usually involving supernatural powers or a secret knowledge of them.

"OUT"—Participating in external life.

PERPETRATOR—A person who abuses another person.

PERSONALITY—A relatively enduring pattern of perceiving and relating to self, others, and the environment. In DID it can refer to any identity exhibiting such a pattern.

PRESENT (verb)—To emerge into external consciousness and take part in life.

PRESENTER—A personality who consistently plays a role in normal daily living.

PRESENTING SYSTEM—The group of personalities who normally handles daily life for the person.

PROGRAM—A predetermined response pattern deliberately established in a person's mind which occurs automatically when triggered by a distinct stimulus.

PROGRAMMING—The entire conglomerate of programs established in a person's mind by a perpetrator group to direct behavior, thoughts, emotions and/or the withholding of information.

RITUAL ABUSE—A systematic form of abuse usually having a predetermined purpose or agenda.

SATANIC CULT—An organized group of people with an established belief system involving the direct or indirect worship of Satan and/or demons and the seeking and exercising of occult powers.

SATANIC RITUAL ABUSE (SRA)—Severe trauma/torture experienced at the hands of a Satanic cult to cause dissociation into multiple personalities so that some of those personalities can be indoctrinated, programmed, and demonized, bringing the individual under the control of the cult and the kingdom of darkness—generally without the knowledge of the Host personality.

SPIRITUAL WARFARE—The utilization of spiritual principles which apply the authority of the Lord Jesus Christ and the power of His shed blood to counteract demonic activity.

SPLIT—To form an alter-identity through dissociation.

SURVIVOR—A person who has been severely abused; a preferred term to "victim."

SWITCH—To change the executive control of the body from one identity to another.

SYSTEM—The entire group of identities within an individual who has Dissociative Identity Disorder; can also be used of a sub-group of identities with a distinct authority structure which functions more or less independently within the whole.

SYSTEM MAP—An internal depiction of the structural arrangement and operational dynamics of all the identities in the system, providing a line of authority and method of presentation or participation in life. The type of imagery used varies greatly (a house, a castle, a solar system, a carousel, a forest, etc.) and is usually distinct for every multiple.

TALK THROUGH—The process by which a therapist (or other person) addresses alters who are not in control of the body or willing to acknowledge their presence but are able to listen to what is said.

TRIGGER—A specific stimulus which causes a given response; frequently one which is deliberately designed to activate a program.

Appendix B

Types of Alter Personalities

CORE—The personality who is most directly related to the whole person conceived in the womb; carries the strongest sense of "self."

*HOST—The presenter personality who is in executive control of the body most of the time.

*PRESENTERS—The group of alters who normally handles daily living; includes the Host.

FUNCTION ALTERS—Alters created to perform specific functions unhindered by the effects of the trauma; often serve as presenters. They may also be formed to "protect" certain talents or encapsulate certain emotions, positive or negative.

VICTIMS—Alters whose sole function was to handle trauma.

CARETAKER—An alter who watches over, and may speak for, very young alters.

PROTECTORS—Alters created to protect the person from any perceived danger and/or further abuse; often intervene to take abuse in place of weaker alters; often carry a lot of anger and can be aggressive.

INNER SELF HELPER (ISH)—An internal alter who is devoted to the good of the person and works to maintain internal stability and well-being; often provides helpful information to guide the therapist.

REPORTER—An alter who serves to keep track of the facts and relate them without emotion; may also be called "narrator," "moderator," "historian," etc.

CONTROLLERS—Alters who determine which alter will come out at a given time to handle a given situation.

PERSECUTORS—Alters who have identified with the motives and agenda of the abuser and punish the other alters, internally (torment) or externally (self-harm), in the absence of the abuser when the alters do not perform as desired.

SHELL—An alter fragment through whom the personalities and perspectives of other alters can present. The resulting "hand in glove" type of presentation serves to maintain a sense of consistent identity and a continuous short-term memory for the individual, thus minimizing the sense of time loss and switching. While the shell functions as the speaker, it usually has no developed personality of its own. Sometimes a shell may serve solely to provide "housing" for a demon, which can then express itself through a human voice.

CULT ALTERS—Alters who participate(d) in cult activities, exhibiting varying degrees of cult loyalty. This general group of alters includes victims, protectors, persecutors, and reporters. In this case, protectors serve to guard cult secrets and critical parts of the system, block therapy, and/or warn the system of any threat to its agenda. Reporters relate the activities of the person back to the cult.

* These can change over the course of a person's life.

Appendix C

Requirements for Types of Support

I. **Emotional Support**

   A. **Knowledge Required**
      1. Basic dynamics of DID/SRA
      2. Principles of spiritual warfare and their unique applications to DID/SRA
      3. Familiarity with typical SRA memories
      4. Familiarity with the survivor's presenting alters
      5. Other resources available to the survivor

   B. **Skills Required**
      1. Being a compassionate listener
      2. Maintaining objectivity
      3. Handling horrific memories and facilitating their healing
      4. Dealing with various types of alters
      5. Confronting demons
      6. Detecting when a survivor may be in danger and need greater help or safety than you can provide

II. Physical Support

A. Knowledge Required
1. Basic dynamics of DID/SRA
2. Principles of spiritual warfare and their unique applications to DID/SRA
3. Familiarity with the main alters of the survivor and their issues
4. The types of harm apt to be attempted and how to prevent them

B. Skills Required
1. Physically, but non-abusively, restraining the survivor when required
2. Calling out particular alters
3. Confronting demons
4. Knowing when additional help is needed

III. Spiritual Support

A. Prayer
1. Knowledge Required
   a. Fundamentals of DID/SRA
   b. Principles of spiritual warfare and their unique applications in DID/SRA
   c. Principles of effective prayer
2. Skills Required
   a. Effective praying
   b. Spiritual warfare

B. Spiritual Warfare

1. Knowledge Required
   a. Fundamentals of DID/SRA
   b. Principles of spiritual warfare and their unique applications in DID/SRA
   c. Spiritual armor
2. Skills Required
   a. Recognition of possible demonic activity or influence
   b. Judicious confrontation of demons
      1). Working to gain cooperation of alters involved
      2). Identifying footholds
      3). Facilitating the renunciation of footholds

C. Discipleship

1. Knowledge Required
   a. Basic dynamics of DID/SRA
   b. Basic doctrines of the Bible
   c. Principles of spiritual warfare and their unique applications to DID/SRA
2. Skills Required
   a. Teaching truth
   b. Modeling truth
   c. Dealing with alter-personalities and demons

IV. Financial Support

No specific requirements

V. Therapeutic Support

A. Personal requirements
1. Significant availability of time
2. Significant emotional stamina
3. Psychological, emotional, and spiritual health
4. Ability to set and maintain healthy personal boundaries
5. Exceptional interpersonal skills
6. Comfortable in dealing with all emotions and personality types
7. Comfortable in dealing with sexual issues
8. Love, sensitivity and compassion

B. Knowledge required
Volunteers for this degree of involvement need an extensive, but not prohibitive, amount of training, preferably in an apprentice-type situation including, but not limited to:
1. Nature of Satanic Ritual Abuse
2. Long-term effects of trauma and sexual abuse
3. Complex dynamics of system structure
4. Role of conflict and denial in DID
5. Conflict resolution dynamics
6. Programming dynamics
7. Demonization issues

C. Skills required
1. Building trust and rapport with alters
2. Identifying key parts of the personality system
3. Resolving crises
4. Doing effective spiritual warfare and deliverance

a. Differentiating alters and demons
   b. Modifying techniques to apply to dissociative dynamics
5. Processing memories
   a. To bring healing to pain
   b. To remove programming
6. Identifying and resolving the psychological conflicts which necessitated dissociation
7. Facilitating integration of alter-identities
8. Teaching healthy living and coping skills

Appendix D

A Plan for Implementing an SRA Support Team within the Local Church

I. **Phase One: Education**

   A. **Objective:** To enable selected church members to decide whether they want to become involved in supporting an SRA survivor

   B. **Method**
   1. A week-end seminar
   2. Weekly workshops

   C. **Content**
   1. Awareness of the extent of the problem
   2. Basic understanding of Satanic cults
      a. Levels of involvement
      b. Belief systems
      c. Ways of operating
         1). Recruiting
         2). Controlling
         3). Programming

3. Basic understanding of dissociation and DID
    a. The mechanism of dissociation
    b. The role of trauma
    c. The process of therapy
    d. Support needs of survivors
4. The nature of the spiritual realm and spiritual warfare
    a. The cosmic conflict between God and Satan
    b. The role of demonization in SRA
    c. The difference between demons and alters
    d. Legal grounds for demonization
    e. Dealing with demons and deliverance

II. Phase Two: Exposure

A. **Objective: To give selected, educated church members the opportunity to see if they feel comfortable dealing with an actual survivor**

B. **Method:**
    1. Video tape of survivor in a therapy session or with a friend as various alters present
    2. Live testimony of a survivor to the group
    3. Personal interaction with a survivor accompanied by a therapist or supporting friend

III. Phase Three: Commitment

A. **Objective: To obtain the commitment of those selected individuals who are willing to become active members of a support group for SRA survivors**

B. **Method: The various aspects of support ministry for SRA survivors should be described with opportunity for individuals to volunteer for involvement in one or more areas.**
    1. Emotional support   (compassionate listening)
    2. Physical support   (safety in times of crisis; assistance in tasks)
    3. Spiritual support   (prayer, discipleship, spiritual warfare)
    4. Financial support   (financial aid)
    5. Therapeutic support (facilitating therapeutic healing)

IV. Phase Four: Training

A. **Objective: To provide any additional training necessary to prepare those committing themselves to a specific area of support**

B. **Additional lectures**
    1. Dealing with alter-personalities and demons
       (Needed for emotional, physical, spiritual, and therapeutic support)
    2. Typical memories and how to process them
       (Needed for emotional and therapeutic support)
    3. Keeping an SRA survivor safe
       (Needed for emotional, physical, spiritual, and therapeutic support)
    4. Spiritual warfare and effectual prayer
       (Needed for all areas)
    5. Others as deemed necessary

C. **Apprenticeship training**
 1. Observing a trained person handling various pertinent situations with a survivor
 2. Performing the same functions under the observation of a trained person
 3. Providing support on your own with a trained person available for consultation

Appendix E

Satanic Calendar

January 7	*St. Winebald's Day*	Blood Rituals
January 17	*Satanic Revels*	Sexual Rituals
*January 20-26	*Sacrificial Preparation for Grand Climax*	
*January 27	*Grand Climax*	Sexual Rituals & Human Sacrifice
February 2	*Candlemas (Sabbat Festival)*	Blood Rituals
February 25	*St. Walpurgis Day*	Blood Rituals
March 1	*St. Eichatadt Day*	Blood Rituals
*March 20/21	*Spring Equinox Feast Day (Sabbat Festival)*	Sexual Rituals
March 21	*Ostara*	Sexual Rituals
*Good Friday	*Day of Passion*	Human Sacrifice
*Easter Eve Day		Human Sacrifice
*April 21-25	*Sacrificial Preparation for Grand Climax*	
*April 26	*Grand Climax*	Sexual & Blood Rituals
April 30	*Roodmas Day, Walpurgis Night*	Sexual & Blood Rituals
May 1	*Beltane, Walpurgis Day*	
	Druid Fire Festival	Coven Initiations
*June 21	*Summer Solstice Feast*	Sexual & Blood Rituals
July 1	*Demon Revels*	Blood Rituals
		Sexual Rituals with Demons
*July 20-26	*Sacrificial Preparation for Grand Climax*	
*July 27	*Grand Climax*	Sexual Rituals & Human Sacrifice
	(5 weeks & 1 day after summer solstice)	
July 31 or August 1	*Lammas Day (Sabbat Festival)*	Sexual & Blood Rituals
August 1	*Lughnasadh*	Sexual Rituals
August 3	*Satanic Revels*	Sexual Rituals
September 7	*Marriage to the Beast*	Sexual Rituals & Infant Sacrifice
September 20	*Midnight Host*	Blood Rituals (Hand of Glory)

September 22	*Autumnal Equinox Feast Day*	Sexual Rituals
October 28	*Satanist High Holy Day*	Human Sacrifices
October 29	*Satanist High Holy Day*	Human Sacrifices
October 30	*Satanist High Holy Day*	Human Sacrifices
October 31	*All Hallows Eve (Samhain)*	Blood & Sexual Rituals with Demons
November 1	*Satanist High Holy Day*	Sexual Rituals & Human Sacrifices
November 4	*Satanic Revels*	Sexual Rituals
December 22	*Winter Solstice Feast Day (Sabbat Festival)*	Sexual Rituals
December 24	*Demon Revels, High Grand Climax*	Blood Rituals
Each New Moon		Blood Rituals
Each Full Moon *Esbat*		Blood and Sexual Rituals

*Birthdays of members
*Birthday of high priest

The Feast of the Beast occurs every 28 years. Last occurred in 1981. Next one due in 2009.

Note: Most feast days begin either at sunset the evening before or at the stroke of midnight.

*Denotes most important dates

ENDNOTES

[1] *Merriam-Webster's Collegiate Dictionary*, 10th ed. (1993), s.v. "Transference."

[2] David Witkovsky, 1997.

[3] Ed Smith of Campbellsville, KY, coined the term "TheoPhostic" (God + Light) to describe this approach to emotional healing. He conducts frequent seminars training both professionals and lay people in using this approach. For more information contact him at Alathia Training Center, P.O. Box 489, Campbellsville, KY 42719, (270) 465-3757.

[4] David Neswald, Lecture at the annual conference of the Christian Society for the Healing of Dissociative Disorders, Dallas, TX, August 1996.

[5] *Diagnostic and Statistical Manual—IV*, 1994, 477.

[6] Ibid., p. 487.

[7] *Passport* Magazine, "America's Best Kept Secret," 1987.